SAGE was founded in 1965 by Sara Miller McCune to support the dissemination of usable knowledge by publishing innovative and high-quality research and teaching content. Today, we publish over 900 journals, including those of more than 400 learned societies, more than 800 new books per year, and a growing range of library products including archives, data, case studies, reports, and video. SAGE remains majority-owned by our founder, and after Sara's lifetime will become owned by a charitable trust that secures our continued independence.

Los Angeles | London | New Delhi | Singapore | Washington DC | Melbourne

DEMOCRATIZING DEVELOPMENT

DEMOCRATIZING DEVELOPMENT
Struggles for Rights and Social Justice in India

Ranjita Mohanty

Los Angeles I London I New Delhi
Singapore I Washington DC I Melbourne

First published in 2018 by

SAGE Publications India Pvt Ltd
B1/I-1 Mohan Cooperative Industrial Area
Mathura Road, New Delhi 110 044, India
www.sagepub.in

SAGE Publications Inc
2455 Teller Road
Thousand Oaks, California 91320, USA

SAGE Publications Ltd
1 Oliver's Yard, 55 City Road
London EC1Y 1SP, United Kingdom

SAGE Publications Asia-Pacific Pte Ltd
3 Church Street
#10-04 Samsung Hub
Singapore 049483

Published by Vivek Mehra for SAGE Publications India Pvt Ltd, typeset in 10/12.5 pt ITC Stone Serif by Zaza Eunice, Hosur, Tamil Nadu, India and printed at Chaman Enterprises, New Delhi.

Library of Congress Cataloging-in-Publication Data Available

ISBN: 978-93-528-0727-7 (HB)

SAGE Team: Rajesh Dey, Guneet Kaur Gulati, Kumar Indra Mishra and Rajinder Kaur.

My father

Rabindra Nath Mohanty

for everything

Thank you for choosing a SAGE product!
If you have any comment, observation or feedback,
I would like to personally hear from you.

Please write to me at **contactceo@sagepub.in**

Vivek Mehra, Managing Director and CEO, SAGE India.

Contents

Preface

The normative idea of progress on which development is fashioned gets vitiated by the power and politics associated with development. The control and distribution of resources, competition among social powers, state intervention and global forces create enclaves of inequality and exclusion. How the poor and socially marginalized, through their struggle for rights and social justice, create conditions for participation, redistribution, equity, equality and inclusion is what this book offers.

The book is positioned in the historical framework of development that India adopted soon after independence from colonial rule. The successive shifts, notwithstanding the framework, have retained, until recently, the core principles of economic development with social justice and the state as the guarantor of development. Even when neoliberal growth projects are pursued ruthlessly, the welfare and social protection projects are not abandoned. The framework has created aspiration, shaped imagination and influenced people's struggles for the democratization of development, even though it has exploited and excluded them. This book shows, when people engage in social struggles to democratize development, they also expand the framework by accepting the desirable and rejecting the undesirable, as well as by providing alternative visions and practices.

The book is set in the Indian villages and contains my research conducted over the last 20 years. Some of my works included in the book were published earlier. I have reworked on them to bring under the theme of the book.

While writing this book, I was struck not only by the complexity of development as it manifests in the Indian villages but also by the complex machinery that works or does not work to deliver development. That the poor, uneducated, socially oppressed and powerless question development shows not only their courage, determination and endurance, but it also shows how the encounter with development has made such struggles an essential part of their living.

Ranjita Mohanty

2 January 2018

Acknowledgements

It is difficult to acknowledge the diverse ways in which so many people over so many years have contributed to make this book possible. I can never thank them enough. I take this occasion to let them know that they have been part of the making of the book.

I had started putting together ideas for this book during my Fulbright year, 2006–07, I spent at the Anthropology Department, University of North Carolina, USA. I am most thankful to Arturo Escobar for clarity, critical ideas and much needed inspiration. The book wouldn't have been possible without him.

Chapters 3 and 4 are based on studies conducted as part of a multi-country research project—the Development Research Centre on Citizenship, Participation and Accountability. I am very thankful to Rajesh Tandon, John Gaventa, Andrea Cornwall, Vera Coelho, Lisa Thompson, Steven Robins, Joanna Wheeler, Mandakini Pant, Bettina von Lieres and others who commented on drafts and with whom I had an opportunity to discuss in workshops. The studies would not have been complete without two people, Ganga Joshi and Tapas Satpathy. They were my constant companions in the field and from whose work in the villages of Uttarakhand and Gujarat I gathered some of the key learnings in social mobilization. Thanks for being with me in work and in leisure.

For Chapter 5, I am most thankful to Gaya Prasad Gopal and Bhagwat Prasad of Akhil Bharatiya Samaj Seva Sansthan, Chitrakoot. I visited the area in 2008. They not only took me to the villages where I had a chance to know about the land rights struggle of the Kol Tribe but also were most helpful in providing many details during subsequent discussions in person and on phone.

The interactions held during fieldwork and conducting workshops, besides many informal conversations, generated ideas that have gone into the book. Space is a limiting factor in naming people individually. Herein I extend thanks to all.

Outside the boundary of work, family and friends have encouraged, indulged, arranged lunches and coffees, skyped from long distances. All of you must know that you have been invaluable.

Last but not the least, my thanks to the editors at SAGE for taking this work forward from the manuscript to a printed volume.

Introduction
Democratizing Development
Issues and Actors

Development was the most enchanting leap of the 20th century that human imagination could take towards the future of mankind. Development as an idea of progress and as a force of modernization promised to take societies from the state of backwardness to progress that involved progress from poverty to prosperity, from disease to health, from illiteracy to literacy and from cultural conservatism to modernity. This transformation called for economic and production systems to be rearranged to maximize economic growth. It was believed that enlarging the size of the economic pie would lead to common prosperity. It was believed that much in the same way as economy could be planned, cultural modernization could also be planned through expert intervention. It was impossible not to get attracted to this model proposed by development.

In the Indian parlance, democracy was added to the model of development by combining economic development with social justice. It envisioned a model which would share economic prosperity with the poor and socially marginalized groups of tribal, Dalits and women, and the economic progress of the marginalized population would alter the landscape of social inequality. Development, combined with democracy, promised *inclusion* of the marginalized in development; it promised *redistribution* of the benefits of development. Development assumed that both the *process* and the *outcome* of development would be democratic.

The history of development shows that the enchanting idea of development has not significantly altered the conditions of the marginalized. There is concentration of wealth and staggering poverty; there is a small pocket of prosperity amid large-scale hunger, malnutrition, disease and illiteracy. The parallel economies of growth projects primarily propelled through industrialization and global trade, and the welfare-oriented poverty eradication projects of land reforms, employment, livelihood, food security and natural resource management have not only come into conflict as they claim the same resources of land, water and forest that constitute the source of livelihood for a large number of the rural population, but they have also affected the marginalized in different ways. If the growth projects have excluded the marginalized from the *process* of decision-making as well as from the *sharing* of the benefits of development, the poverty eradication projects have created difficulties in *access* to benefits. The process and the outcome both have become *undemocratic*. Both *procedural justice* and *distributive justice* have suffered. The undemocratic aspects of development, however, are not accepted passively by the marginalized. This book shows how people protest, claim, question and negotiate to counter what is undemocratic in development and how they infuse development with inclusion, equality, redistribution and equity.

The question, how democratic or undemocratic has development been, gives rise to more questions: How development is designed? Who gets the benefits and who is deprived? Who is included and who is excluded? How are developmental provisions accessed? Who gets access? What are the terms and conditions of access? Who controls development? Why does development result in empowerment and agency in certain contexts and contrary practices in other? Why are certain aspects of development contested? Why does development designed as a transformative force result in conflict and violence?

Engaging with the questions reveals that the normative idea of development as a transformative force has been subverted by multiple centres of power and politics associated with development that control the resources and appropriate the benefits. Development envisions transformation of the objective conditions in the social relationships through which people live. However, when development interacts with the contexts which are rife with social hierarchies and economic inequalities, it sheds the purity of its design and assumes a political overtone. The footprints of development dispersed across the villages in India over the decades tell the stories of what happens to the modernizing narrative of development when it comes in contact with people in their village settings. People come to experience development as it manifests in different sites. They participate in the village meetings designed by the welfare projects in one site even as they protest in a different site where powerful industries displace them from their land and habitat. They trust the promise of redistribution even as they struggle against the powerful feudal forces to get land rights. Even the same policies and projects can have differential access and outcome at different sites depending on the local contexts of power and dominance as well as intervention by development bureaucracy. People thus struggle arduously to save their livelihoods, to seek access to subsidized food, employment and work, and access to many other developmental provisions such as a house promised by the state. Some people emerge with a set of success stories that tell of their triumph and inclusion in development. Others have stories of discontent, denial of access and exclusion from the schemes designed for them.

If the powers having their genesis in society, economy and politics align and subvert the democratic agenda of development, the powerless do not accept it quietly. They resist both through large-scale and localized protests. They mobilize and make claims through the institutions of the state as much as they articulate their demands in the sphere of civil society. The landscape of development thus does not remain tranquil but becomes a contested domain. The struggles of the marginalized not only articulate public good that lie at the heart of development but also bring to the surface issues of rights and social justice that include a gamut of issues such as inclusion, participation, distribution, redistribution, equity and equality that determine the democratic nature of development. This explains why development does not guarantee much to the poor and powerless unless they themselves work to make development democratic, and why democratization of development is of immense importance to people whom development tries to alienate and bypass.

The book examines the two dominant streams of development—economic growth and welfare-oriented poverty eradication—and engages with the aforementioned questions and issues through the lens of the poor and socially marginalized groups. For people who occupy the lowest rung of the socio-economic hierarchy, democratization of development is saving the resources of land, forest and water on which they subsist from being taken away by growth projects as well as accessing what development promises to them through welfare schemes. It is asserting the existing rights and articulation of new rights. It is about putting social justice squarely at the centre of development discourse. The struggles for rights and social justice point out precisely where development becomes undemocratic; where development as a force for economic and social modernization fails. They also point out how to infuse development with democratic principles. Democratization of development shows what the marginalized groups imagine development to be, and that this imagination is shaped by the promises development makes. In their struggle to democratize development, people not only address what is problematic in the existing models of development but also create new models, form new relations and show new paths to be followed. Democratization also expands the horizon of development by bringing in elements that are critical but seldom constitute part of its vocabulary. Two such elements that, as the book shows, have emerged from attempts to democratize development are non-violence and dignity.

A recurrent theme of development that lends urgency to its democratization is that despite setbacks and defeats, the poor look up to the government-sponsored programmes to rescue them from the traps of poverty, ill health and illiteracy. Sometimes they find alternative ways to survive by creating collective community resources through self-help. For a majority, however, the state is the source of development. People mobilize in diverse ways to put pressure on the state: They protest, they work in collaboration with the state and they negotiate. Social mobilization, as the book demonstrates, has been instrumental in democratizing development.

The Idea of Development

Development is founded on the philosophical idea of progress, which is at once an ethical and rational marker of progression along which a society must move. As sociologist Teodor Shanin puts it succinctly in his essay on 'The Idea of Progress', and I quote at length,

> The core of the concept, and its derivations and the images attached to it, have been overwhelmingly simple and straight-forward. With a few temporary deviations, all societies all advancing naturally and consistently 'up', on a route from poverty, barbarianism, despotism and ignorance to riches, civilization, democracy, and rationality, the highest expression of which is science. This is also an irreversible movement from an endless diversity of particularities, wasteful human energies and economic resources, to a world unified and

simplified into most rational arrangements; it is therefore a movement from badness to goodness and from mindlessness to knowledge, which gave this message its ethical promise, its optimism and its reformist 'punch'. (Shanin 1997, 65)

[The idea of progress] penetrated all strata of contemporary societies to become the popular common sense, and as such resistant to change. Consequently, even when some actual experience challenged that vision (as it often did), such evidence was usually brushed aside as accidental or transitional while the belief in progress and its implications held firm. The wordings changed with fashion: 'progress', 'modernization', 'development', 'growth', and so on. (Shanin 1997, 66)

The Industrial Revolution in Britain was the first concrete manifestation of progress when the rationality of technology and science changed the agrarian society into an industrial one and defined economic prosperity. Almost a century later, the idea echoed in the inaugural speech of the US President Harry S. Truman in 1949:

We must embark on a bold new program for making the benefits of our scientific advances and industrial progress available for the improvement and growth of underdeveloped areas. More than half the people of the world are living in conditions approaching misery. Their food is inadequate. They are victims of disease. Their economic life is primitive and stagnant. Their poverty is a handicap and a threat both to them and to more prosperous areas. For the first time in history, humanity possesses the knowledge and skill to relieve suffering of these people. The United States is preeminent among nations in the development of industrial and scientific techniques. The material resources which we can afford to use for assistance of other peoples are limited. But our imponderable resources in technical knowledge are constantly growing and are inexhaustible.... With the cooperation of business, private capital, agriculture, and labor in this country, this program can greatly increase the industrial activity in other nations and can raise substantially their standards of living.... Greater production is the key to prosperity and peace. And the key to greater production is a wider and more vigorous application of modern scientific and technical knowledge.

Development prescribed industrial production as the most desirable mode of production, which along with the use of science and technology, promised material growth and well-being of individuals and societies. Gross national product based on goods and services produced for consumption by a nation became the indicator of development. Development, as Truman (1949) articulated, divides societies based on their level of development. The North, which is developed, modernized and progressive, has become the model for the South, which is considered underdeveloped and backward, to follow.

The idea of development thus envisions a society's linear movement along a defined path from backwardness to modernity, illiteracy to literacy, irrationality to rationality, diseased to healthy and so on. Development aims to erase diversity in heteronomous societies and promote homogenization (Escobar 1995). It aspires to be universalized in space and promises to be durable in time (Sachs 1997). Development formulates its own concepts, theories, plans and designs. Development requires a set of institutions and experts that can plan and execute the progress of a society (Escobar 1995). Nation states are the units that development seeks to transform. In recent times, globalization has made the boundaries of nation states porous, and not only global capital but also global institutions have made their entry into societies that hitherto managed their development in relative independence.

Positioning Development: Significant Shifts

Despite political upheavals and changing political regimes, development has continued unabated, although certain shifts have taken place within the broad framework of development.

First, as globalization was ushered in and India liberalized its economy in the 1990s, the socialist rhetoric was dropped from the state lexicon of development, and economic growth assumed an aggressive posture. The rise of the global market, on the one hand, implied that the 'nation state' was no longer the unit to be developed, independent of the rest of the world, and, on the other, the entry of external capital and rise of the private sector eroded the size and power of the public sector as the mover of economic growth. With the gradual erosion of state power, industrial development slipped away from the hands of the state and moved to the corporates including the multinationals. Second, while the power of the state in deciding economic growth was reduced, popularized in often quoted remarks, 'the state has no business to do business', the state is still the negotiator of social contract between industry and community. It is the responsibility of the state administration to acquire land for industrial ventures, and often land acquisition itself becomes a contentious issue as it displaces people from their homes and livelihood pursuits. Third, while the state has embraced neoliberalism, it has not abandoned its welfare orientation completely. The state has been at the centre of promoting livelihood, food security, education, health and housing for the poor. Fourth, development is now more vigorously linked with governance, that is, with the performance of the state. While the World Bank's good governance prescriptions— transparency, accountability, rule of law—are criticized as mere administrative reforms, other agencies such as Department for International Development[1] have brought a rights-based approach to development by laying emphasis on citizen rights and citizen action, thus creating possibilities for people to engage with the state in claiming development provisions of goods and services. Fifth, with the enactment of decentralized participatory governance in the form of institutions called panchayat, all state-sponsored development projects are converged at the village level, and are being implemented by panchayats

[1] The international aid agency of the United Kingdom.

with assistance from various government agencies. These new institutions of governance have become sites where development politics of who gets access to development provisions and who remains outside is negotiated and contested by social groups. Sixth, civil society organizations (CSOs), mostly non-governmental organizations (NGOs), are now at the forefront of development collaboration with the state.

While NGOs as voluntary organizations have been addressing the issues of the poor and marginalized social groups, they have functioned by remaining outside the state domain. In their new role as partners with the state, they have become an extended arm of the state in delivering development. The NGOs are now visible in policy formulation, implementation of government projects and building capacity of the communities to access policy benefits. Last but not the least, even as the state has designed ambitious resource-intensive poverty eradication projects and have devolved development to the village level, its economic growth agenda is now contested by the rural inhabitants.

Planned Development: The Indian Story

The Planning Commission established in 1950 was entrusted with the 'responsibility of making assessment of all resources of the country, augmenting deficient resources, formulating plans for the most effective and balanced utilisation of resources and determining priorities' (Planning Commission 1951). The First Five Year Plan was targeted for the period 1951–56. Between the First Plan and the Twelfth Plan (2012–17), there have been shifts in designing and implementing development, although the central motif of development as a model for economic development and social justice has remained unaltered. Multiple streams of development ranging from industrial growth to community-based poverty eradication, natural resource generation to social welfare and livelihood planning to service delivery have been designed to promote development.

The Indian State has remained at the helm of development as a planner, resource allocator and implementer of development.

Industrial development rolled out in India with Prime Minister Nehru's iconic statement while inaugurating the Bhakra Nangal Dam,'Dams are the temples of modern India'. That statement itself shows the immense faith and reverence development commanded at that time. Industrial growth has remained the main architect of development; other poverty eradication projects are designed to provide livelihood support to the poor, protect their ecological resource base and redistribute the resources such as land to the landless and marginal farmers.

Big dams, such as Bhakra Nangal and Hirakud, steel plants in Rourkela, Bhilai and Durgapur, and National Thermal Power Corporation (NTPC) signalled the early phase of industrial growth with the public sector at the helm. Large-scale mining, mechanized fishery and commercial forestry soon began to take shape. Under neoliberal economy, industrialization has received added impetus in the form of demarcation of economic zones and special economic zones (SEZs) to promote industrial growth.

The economic growth agenda since its inception in the First Five Year Plan in 1950 has acknowledged that the benefits will be first appropriated by the rich and will slowly trickle down to the poor. The Eleventh Five Year Plan (2007–12) also mentioned the trickle-down effect and laid emphasis on inclusive growth to include those who were left out or remained at the margins of economic development.

The poverty eradication projects aim to provide livelihoods to the poor who are deprived of the benefits of economic growth and thus contain an implicit or explicit welfare orientation. The Integrated Rural Development Programme and Swarnjayanti Gram Swarojgar Yojana attempted to bring the poor under credit-based programmes for livelihood generation. Credit-based programmes have found a renewed vigour in livelihood projects planned under the National Rural Livelihood

Mission (NRLM) that lays special emphasis on women entrepreneurship in the form of saving and credits popularly known as micro-credit. The National Food Security Act (NFSA) and Public Distribution System (PDS) aimed at providing subsidized food items, such as rice, wheat and sugar, to the poor have welfare and social protection at their core. The most ambitious poverty eradication programme is Mahatma Gandhi National Rural Employment Guarantee Act (MGNREGA/NREGA), a rights-based demand-driven approach to rural employment and sustainable livelihood assets creation for the poor and socially marginalized.

Natural resource regeneration aims to tackle poverty through ecological conservation and management of resources such as soil, water and forest on which village communities subsist. Since the 1970s, regeneration of natural resources has emerged as a strategy to address rural poverty. Forestry and watersheds programmes which focus on the regeneration of forests, water resources, land reclamation and soil conservation are designed to augment the rural economy.

The twin agenda of economic growth and poverty eradication are marked by certain contradictions and conflicts between the two that are as follows:

1. The industry and service sector has been the main contributor to growth measured in terms of gross domestic product. Agriculture on which a large number of people in rural areas are dependent for their livelihood has been witnessing a slow growth. While agriculture has received policy attention to augment the food supply in the 1960s and 1970s, industrial growth has been prioritized post globalization. Large swaths of agriculture land are diverted to industries.
2. The resources of land, water and forest are claimed by both the growth projects as well as the poverty eradication projects. The state, however, gives priority to commercial interests than people's subsistence interests. Hence, while prime agricultural land is given to industries, the poverty

eradication projects try to improve the degraded land to make it cultivable for the poor.
3. While the planning and execution of growth-oriented projects have proceeded without people's participation, particularly from those who are adversely affected by them, the institutions of decentralized governance have been reinvigorated to elicit participation in development programmes implemented through the decentralized institutions of panchayat.

The Politics of Development

The modernizing project of development is linear, and development seeks to foster a universal and homogenous culture among populations who constitute the objects of development across the developing world. The linearity and homogeneity of development emanate from its belief that societies and cultures require following a prescribed path to become 'developed'. Development is thus designed with technocratic precision to eliminate social inequalities and competition among the social groups for resources. Development, however, neglects the micro contexts of villages where it is executed. Hence, despite its neatness of articulation and the desire to implement such neatness through a network of institutions and experts, development loses its sophistication and clarity precisely at the moment when it comes in contact with the population it is expected to develop, for that is exactly when the politics of development surfaces and becomes apparent.

From the point of view of technologies of development, development appears an easy task. However, development does not submit itself to a technocratic exercise. What might appear as a simple task, selection of beneficiaries, for example, through an enumeration of below poverty line (BPL) households, becomes complex and contested as much manipulation goes into the listing of households. Since getting into the list gives access to development resources, even households that are not poor compete to get themselves listed. Likewise, village institutions formed for participation become spaces for competition and conflict that subvert the participation of the marginalized. Social groups such as the Dalits, women and tribals often find themselves outside the decision-making process. The local bureaucracy, the prime agency that has administrative expertise and technical knowledge to deliver development, tries to retain its control over people and often creates a nexus of social and administrative powers. In fact, policies, in many instances, are sabotaged at these micro-spheres of the state (Mohanty 2014). But technologies of development do not acknowledge this. Development is viewed and planned with the precision of science that can counter any hurdle to achieve its goal because the goal is a logical one. Despite a technologically sophisticated tool known as management information system (MIS) that is used to monitor the progress of a development project, there are instances of financial corruption, wrong entry of beneficiaries and entry of activities that are either not undertaken or left incomplete. Even technology is manipulated by the politics of development.

At the heart of the development paradox lies the conception of both private good (creation of household assets such as a house or credit for starting a business) and public good (creation of common resources such as health care or PDS delivery through ration shops or drinking water supply) as universally accepted and therefore uncontested. Such a conception of private/public good suggests that the rich will let the poor have the material resources, men will be quite happy to share decision-making with women, upper castes will be willing to sit on the same platform with the Dalits, and the state will be neutral in dealing with its citizens. However, it does not happen that way. Development scholars and practitioners have documented the 'politics', understood as contestation over power and resources, that affects development. Ironic as it may sound, development promises to wipe out inequalities, but wants to remain apolitical.

Ferguson (1990) from his study in Lesotho shows how the development discourse is depoliticized by confining its success or failure to bureaucratic performance and how development experts steer clear from the messy terrain of politics and make development as a technocratic design sans the 'vernacular and intelligible'. Development by intent and design is conceived as technocratic, rational and apolitical. However, when technically managed development interacts with people on the ground, it gets politicized. The subsequent chapters will show how socially marginalized groups challenge and fight against the local currents to make development both equitable and accessible.

Development and the State

The history of Indian development reveals that the state, as the prime mover of development, has always remained at the helm of affairs. The state is an everyday presence in the lives of the poor and socially vulnerable. As codified power, ultimate decision-maker and resource mobilizer, the state impinges on the lives of people more than any other force, thereby determining how affairs in society are to be managed. While under neoliberalism the public sector gives way to the private sector and foreign capital, the state still controls the social contract between industry and society. The movements against Vedanta[2] and POSCO,[3] two international mining companies, have pitched the struggle vis-à-vis the state. Notwithstanding the retreat of the state under a globalized and liberalized economy, its presence in the arenas of social welfare and social justice is still central. NREGA, Right to Information Act and NFSA are landmark policies, and they not only signify the presence of the state, but also shape people's expectations.

[2] Vedanta Aluminium Limited is a part of Vedanta Resources, a conglomerate of companies. Its headquarters is based in London.
[3] POSCO is a Korean mining company.

Another aspect of the state that signifies its presence is decentralized local governance. The institutions of local governance are mandated by the Constitution to promote economic development and social justice. All development programmes are executed by the local institutions called panchayat. Participation and democracy in the state-sponsored development programmes are thus intended to be pursued through the institutional mechanism of panchayat. The decentralized local governance has not only brought the state closer to people but has also made the state a source of social power. This has given rise to competition and conflict among the social groups for power on the one hand, and a new kind of citizen politics by the poor that is located in the state arena, on the other. Although such institutions are often co-opted or rendered helpless by powerful industrial forces that grab land without involving the local institutions, the Supreme Court's direction in 2013 in the case of Vedanta mining operations in the Niyamgiri Hills in Odisha has energized gram sabha[4] as the ultimate decision-making forum for land acquisition in tribal areas.

To understand the significance of the state, it is important to understand the nature of the post-colonial state and the depth of people's relationships of dependence and patronage with it. It is important to understand how the state features in the imagination of people since it is their relationship with the state, ranging from disillusionment and despair to seeing it as a patron and a benefactor, which is reflected in their relationship with the state. As Chandhoke (2005, 1037) puts it, 'political preferences for the state over other actors are the outcome of historical processes... that preference formation takes place in a historical context, that of specific institutions or systems of rules. These shape interest, fix responsibility and guide the formation of expectations'. The resourceless people continue to look up to the state to intervene and solve their problem. For

---

[4] A gram sabha consists of all adult residents in a village or a number of villages that make a panchayat. The gram sabha members elect the panchayat representatives.

historical reasons the state still looms large in the perception of millions of people.

Poor people's relation with the state is often complex and ambiguous. Take for example, a situation where people who protest economic growth projects in the form of SEZs are also the beneficiaries of the anti-poverty programme, NREGA. Here they protest one set of state action, but they are dependent on another set of state action for patronage and welfare. Their relation with the state is thus far from perfect; the state is indispensable, but it is also inadequate (Hansen and Stepputat 2001). The state can be authoritarian, but it is also a source of patronage and welfare. How people see the state and how the state comes across to people is contextual (Corbridge et al. 2005) and depends on which agency of the state is closer to them in their daily interaction; it could be the Border Security Force or a block development officer (BDO). People thus have multiple and often conflicting images of the state—the same state that enacts the right to food security of the poor also takes away their land for industrial growth. The giver of rights becomes the destroyer of livelihoods.

The state is at once a distant impersonal idea as well as a localized and personified institution (Gupta 2001). The distant idea gives rise to an imaginary ideal state people would like to have, but the personified institutions of the state are often a source of anxiety. Since the post-colonial states came into power after prolonged periods of radical nationalist struggle, their origin makes them benevolent in the eyes of their populace. However, as the post-colonial states continue to fashion themselves after the power structures and motives of the colonial state, their actual behaviour is often different from how they are idealized by the poor.

Governmentality of development is thus a tenuous affair that involves different facets of the state and their institutional settings, intentions, discourses and strategies vis-à-vis citizens. From policy formulations that take place at the highest level of the state to their implementation through a vast network of bureaucracy from district downwards, the manifestations of the state are diverse and at times in conflict with each other.

The historical context of evolution of the particular forms of political order gives rise to particular forms of social manifestation of aspiration and discontent. For example, the land reforms initiated in the 1960s and 1970s for distribution of free land to landless and marginal farmers as a measure to ensure social justice points out to a form of socialist and democratic orientation of the political order. As such when people made demands on the state to fulfil those aspirations, the state evaded in the beginning, but it could not bypass the demands completely. Contrast this with the economic growth agenda of the state, for example, mining. Here the state goes to any extent to take away livelihood resources of the poor without any information or deliberation. It invokes the 'public good' argument that entitles the state to take land for what it considers as the national good. In this context, the political order is no longer socialist or even democratic, but of a neoliberal market economy in which the state assumes the role of a global player. Resistance to such state action by citizens often invokes suppression and violence from the state.

The state is deeply embedded in the social settings in which it operates. The larger social context at times sabotages progressive actions from the state. For example, institutions that are created by the state to mobilize Dalits, women and tribal communities to participate in development are often sabotaged by the social settings in which they function. Dominant castes often sabotage Dalit issues, and patriarchy often sabotages women's issues, thus restricting their participation. In such contexts, even when the state is close to Dalits and women by virtue of its location in their own village/block/district,[5] the state, in many instances, instead of allying with the marginalized social groups, makes alliance with the dominant social forces. There

[5] The decentralized system of governance is a three-tier system that begins at villages, has blocks as middle-level administrative arrangements and ends at districts.

are, however, contrary evidences when the state allies with the poor and such alliances more often than not take place due to the will of individual officials rather than state institutions.

Development and Civil Society

Development is not the domain exclusive to the state. Present in the sphere of development are actors in civil society—the sphere that lies outside the formal boundary of the state. Actions in civil society do both, resist the state and support it: Civil society actions support the state where support is required for the state to implement development that serves the interest of people; on the other hand, when the interests of the state clash with people's interest, the state faces resistance from civil society.

There were no major stirrings in the social sphere for almost two decades after independence due to what is euphemistically called the phase of 'nation-building'. Since the state assumed the role of provider, protector and regulator, there was faith that the state would deliver. People believed that the state was not only responsible for development but also possessed the expertise and resources and had systems for leading them towards progress and prosperity. The voluntary organizations inspired by the Gandhian ideology of rural reconstruction dotted the landscape of civil society. In this form, civil society was supportive of the state.

As the years progressed, it became increasingly clear that the state had not been able to live up to its democratic promises. The democratic state that was formed after freedom from the colonial rule was expected to remain an independent and autonomous actor that would reform society, create opportunities for the poor and promote growth, but would remain above the diversity, complexities and divisiveness of Indian society. By the 1960s, it became clear that the state had compromised on its role as an independent actor leading to the subversion of the socio-economic transformation agenda by the same forces against which it was planned. The landed elite, the industrial class and the upper castes—historically placed in a dominant position—put pressure on the state and appropriated developmental benefits thereby undermining the purpose of both development and democracy (Bardhan 1984, 1988; Dhanagre 1987; Kohli 1987, 1988; Kothari 1986).

The 1970s marked the emergence of social movements in India. The Naxalite Movement in West Bengal mobilized the poor peasantry to demand land reforms; the Chipko Movement in Uttaranchal mobilized women to protect the forests against commercial encroachment; and Sampoorn Kranti, literally translated as 'total revolution', mobilized cross sections of citizenry to critique the very foundation of governance that had turned in favour of the ruling elites. The decade of the 1970s was also significant because it witnessed a shift in the nature of the Indian State, a shift that led to the redefinition of the relationship between civil society and the State. The National Emergency declared in 1975 by the ruling Congress party was in operation for 19 months (June 1975–March 1977), during which the democratic rights were suspended. Declared on 25 June 1975, against a backdrop of social and political agitations, the Emergency revealed the hidden potential of democratic state to turn dictatorial. The state of emergency and the subsequent restoration of democracy not only redefined and extended the boundaries of civil society by redefining the relationship of the citizens with the state, they also restructured civil society in a significant way and made it more alert to transgressions of its boundary by the state. The post-Emergency period witnessed the formation of civil liberty and human rights organizations such as People's Union for Civil Liberty.

Civil society space began to be filled by voluntary development organizations (NGOs) that came up in the 1970s and 1980s to address the issues of ecology, education, health, housing and livelihood. The organizations have occupied the space at grassroots as well as at provincial and national levels. They differ in their mode of addressing development. Some engage in advocacy with the government to change the existing development policies or for the formulation of new policies; some mobilize grassroots communities to demand their rights and entitlements through the implementation of existing policies. Organizations have also promoted alternative arrangements of livelihood and local economy, and education and health care facilities in areas where the state action is either absent or inadequate.

The advent of neoliberalism in the opening years of the 1990s has significantly altered the relationship between the civil society and the state. On the one hand, there is a kind of collaborative relationship between the two which is new in its form, content and magnitude. The state has opened itself up to work with that part of the civil society that is willing to work with it. CSOs[6] are invited to take part in the formulation of development policies and implementation of state-sponsored development programmes. The state has sought collaboration with CSOs in supporting social mobilization among the beneficiary communities to enable them to access developmental provisions. CSOs also support the state in conducting social audit—a process through which social groups hold the state officials accountable. CSO support is also sought for the revitalization of participatory institutions formed under decentralized governance. CSOs thus support the state in creating awareness and mobilizing marginalized social groups to participate in panchayat activities either as elected representative or as gram sabha members. However, while the state has been decentralized and it has been building collaborations with civil society actors to bring efficiency and effectiveness in development and governance, it is coming down heavily on social movements opposing the state-driven projects of economic growth that

---

[6] The 1990s changed the nomenclature of voluntary organizations/ NGOs to CSOs. As civil society became a buzzword following the downfall of authoritarian regimes in Eastern Europe, Africa and Latin America, where people standing in the sphere of civil society had acted against the state, the donor agencies created programmes for supporting civil societies. This led the NGOs refer themselves as CSOs.

have reached a new zenith with the liberalization of economy to foreign investment.

The Politics of Development: The Politics of Knowledge and Power

Despite its technological rationality and proclaimed value neutrality, the very model of development contains within it the politics of knowledge and power. At the transnational level, development celebrates the knowledge and power of the West/North over the developing world of the South. Within the boundaries of the nation state, development gives primacy of knowledge and power of the state over its people. At the micro-level of the villages where it is actually implemented, the knowledge and power of the dominant groups and local bureaucracy influence development.

Informed by the lived experiences of people, multiple discourses of development and practices have surfaced to contest this politics of knowledge and power. The dominance of knowledge, interests and relations that development serves at the cost of the exclusion of the poor and marginalized social groups generated much debate during the early stages of development as grassroots movements and activists in many developing countries began articulating the discontents, exclusion and violence of development.[7] These articulations urged development to acknowledge the existence of multiple realities, and realities as context specific. They urged development to value poor people's knowledge and practice.

Two schools of thought and practice emerged in the developing countries where the discontents of development were visible and where these new articulations were taking place. Participatory development influenced by the Brazilian educator Paulo Freire's principles of conscientization and empowerment

[7] Ecology and women's movements articulated this position in India.

put emphasis on people's knowledge and their ability to reflect and act. The discourses of participatory development and alternative development have sought to address the issues of knowledge and power, albeit in different ways. Participatory development has brought Freire's notion of popular knowledge into the domain of development. It has attempted to counter mainstream developmental assumptions that the poor are ignorant and backward, and therefore, need outside expert knowledge for development. It urges development to value people's knowledge and practice and to engage them in the identification of their problems and consider their own solutions to their problems rather than development experts listing the problems and solutions for the beneficiaries.[8] This has found resonance among many activists and organizations in India working among farmers, fishermen and women.

Alternative development informed by grassroots groups working on ecological issues equates poverty in the developing countries with the ecological fallouts of development. It articulates an alternative development model based on local ecological knowledge and argues that such knowledge is required for the sustenance of ecological resources and for the sustainability of development in the long run (Agarwal 1985; Bandopadhyay and Shiva 1988; Bhatt 1991). Alternative development critiques the state for creating an enclave of prosperity for a section of people at the cost of poverty of the vast majority caused by the commercialization of ecological resources of land, water and forest on which poor people subsist. The authoritarian foundation of the state–society relations has received some attention from alternative development as it speaks about the authoritarian tendencies of the state in creating hegemonic relationships and keeping the bulk of the population under poverty. However, as alternative development keeps its focus on engaging the communities in building ecologically sustainable development, it does not expand the alternative relationship

[8] This tradition gave rise to participatory research as a method of research and action (Tandon 2002).

people could have with the state. Alternative development has informed the struggles of the poor against resource-intensive industrialization. The struggles against big dams, mines and commercial forestry in their early years in the 1970s and 1980s articulated alternative economic development that would protect the ecological resources.

The mainstream development regime has adopted some of these articulations and practices although often not in the same form and spirit in which they were articulated. Participatory development found three distinct manifestations in the official discourse: (a) Robert Chamber's participatory rural appraisal is developed as a quick method of rapid appraisal to identify the needs of the poor through a process of community engagement; (b) Amartya Sen's human development and capability approach has added human development indicators to development and has espoused for the capacity enhancement of poor people so that they can make developmental choices; and (c) development projects for poverty eradication, such as forestry and watershed projects, have added to their designs participatory institutions such as users group, village institutions and women's groups to engage people in planning, decision-making as well as in the implementing the projects.

At the grassroots level, the shift has been radical. As grassroots movements contest the ruthless economic growth promoted by neoliberalism instead of alternative development, they now articulate *alternative to development*. This shift is quite visible among social movements in India. During the 1970s and 1980s, the movements opposing big dams, mining, power plants, etc., were concerned about the resettlement and rehabilitation of people affected by projects. The movements articulated alternative ways of development that could reduce human, social and ecological costs. As the neoliberal restructuring of the economy took place, economic growth assumed an unprecedented aggressiveness. The movements in recent times have to contest mining by global companies as well as economic zones promoted by the state to facilitate economic growth. Negotiations for resettlement and rehabilitation are no longer a viable strategy in the context of land acquisition and displacement. The movements at the forefront of opposing international capital are opposing the very model of development. This post-development discourse not only rejects the existing model of development as a source for progress but also the idea of progress on which development is based is discarded (Escobar 1995; Esteva and Prakash 1999; Gibson-Graham 2006).[9] Post-development articulates the re-visioning of a different world based on solidarity and mutuality instead of exclusion and dominance. The social movements resisting global capital across the world and the collective economies the poor are creating for themselves are providing this new vision of development.

Violence of Development

Marikana, the site of British company Lonmin's platinum mine in South Africa, became a site of clashes between the mine workers demanding a raise in their wages and the state oppression that manifested in its most brutal form on 16 August 2012 when the police killed 34 mine workers. The sites of protests in Kashipur and Kalinga Nagar in Odisha and Nandigram in West Bengal have witnessed physical violence by the state to eliminate the protesters. On 16 December 2006, three people were killed in a police firing in Maikanch village, Kashipur when the police took to extremes of violence to suppress the local resistance to Utkal Alumina International Limited (UAIL). On 2 January 2006, the police fired at the people protesting against the Tata Steel SEZ in Kalinganagar killing 12 tribal people. On 14 March 2007, the police killed 13 people protesting against the proposed SEZ for Salim Group of Chemicals in Nandigram,

[9] The post-development argument that 'another world is possible' is made collectively and globally by the World Social Forum which is a network of movements and activists opposing capitalism and globalization.

West Bengal. What these incidents indicate is that the state can take away the lives of people to protect development, particularly to protect the interests of industrial capital. Such state violence in India is evident particularly in contexts where the protests have opposed rapid and ruthless land acquisition by private companies for their industrial projects. A closer look at the spectrum of violence from the state side to deal with protests reveals that while it is usually not willing to concede to critics, it is most brutal when the critics question the economic growth agenda of the state. The violence of development, particularly in neoliberal times, goes unnoticed by the supporters of growth, for growth is touted globally as the redeemer of poverty even though it eliminates the poor in the process.

Violence of development, however, does not stop once it claims the lives of the poor. It is pervasive and surfaces in forms that do not always result in the elimination of lives but do result in threats of physical violence, denial of access to the benefits of development or forceful exclusion from development. Violence takes place whenever the interests of entrenched powers are threatened. Violence in such instances subverts the transformatory potential of development. Let me illustrate this with two examples from development projects that appear quite non-threatening. A programme such as NREGA claims to uplift the poor from poverty traps through a rights-based approach to work. But when such rights are claimed by the poor, they upset the local equations of power centred around cheap and exploitative labour that big farmers and private contractors avail without bargain. NREGA also threatens the local bureaucracy whose manipulation of financial resources can be exposed through social audit provisions contained in the NREGA. There are instances when activists mobilizing rural people to claim their right to work are killed mysteriously.[10] Another example is again the seemingly non-threatening PDS for subsidized food for the poor. The PDS has been marred by

[10] http://www.rtiindia.org/forum/4532-nrega-activist-shot-dead.html

irregularity in shop timings, low quality and irregular supply of food items and supply of lesser quantity than prescribed per person under the PDS. The nexus between the dealers who run the subsidized food outlets called ration shops and the bureaucracy that has the power to give permission to select dealers is strong as it is a common practice to hoard the PDS items and sell at a higher price in the open market. The nexus is so strong that the beneficiaries of the scheme are at the receiving end of violence, including the physical threat that ensues when they make claims for their fair share of subsidized food items.[11]

A question arises at this point whether development is inherently violent or the violence of the state and society gets transferred to development. Not all aspects of development are violent, and it is not that the state only governs by means of violence. However, both development and the state carry within them the potential for violence. The growth agenda of development thus incites violence of both the state and development where they collaborate to fulfil the agenda of capital. In less volatile contexts, such as welfare-oriented development, violence does not emanate from development per se, but it surfaces when the state, the executor of development, becomes an ally of vested power interests. Where power interests are entrenched and any transformation threatens to disturb the existing patterns in favour of the poor and socially deprived, the retaliation is often in the form of violence. In such situations, the state seldom chooses to curb violence; it either remains indifferent or actively supports it through its alliance with local powers.

The violence of development is also the violence of culture. What development alters is not only the economic resource base of the poor but also their culture and ways of living. Development requires people to learn new ways of living that is essentially based on the disruption of old behaviour, social arrangements and economic pursuits. What, for example,

[11] An activist seeking information about the functioning of the ration shops under PDS was physically attacked (Mohanty 2014).

happens when a farmer is forced to become an industrial labourer? Without any formal skill to work in the factories, the peasant can only be absorbed as an unskilled or, with some training, as a semi-skilled labour. The setting of life changes from rural to urban, the ways of living changes from living a life among ones' own people on one's own land to living with migrants in urban slums. Driving people out of their natural habitat to work in the factory and live in slums is one of the cruellest fallouts of development. In planning parlance, it is praised as the generation of employment. But what the planners do not understand is that the jobs they want to create are not always alternatives to the livelihoods they destroy. Development destroys the 'dignity' in pursuing livelihood. A small farmer, a carpenter, a fisherman or an artisan may be poor, but there is a dignity in pursing their livelihoods because they are the masters of their trade. Development does not care what happens to people when they are forced to enter another occupation, live in another place and lead a life that is unknown to them. Development does not recognize the loss of culture and the loss of self that takes place when culture is disrupted. Development creates and writes its own history on the lost history of the culture it destroys. As Nandy (2003, 172) puts it,

> The often violent retooling of the self has gone hand-in-hand with the loss of large parts of the remembered past. Today, only that past is being celebrated which is seen as conducive to modernisation and development; only that past is being rued which seems to resist modernity and development. Together, the two 'relevant' pasts constitute history and become, after a time, the only memory accessible to the citizenry.

The chapters in the book are organized in the following manner:

Chapter 2 discusses the social movements that contest economic growth and their contribution in highlighting the absence of democracy in development. The grassroots movements against big dams, commercial forestry, power projects and mining address the issues of land, livelihood and habitat of the poor destroyed by the ruthless pursuit of economic growth. The chapter argues that the contestations over development shape development to be democratic, for they raise the questions of equity, equality and inclusion.

Chapter 3 discusses the dynamics of exclusion and inclusion of the poor in NREGA, and why inclusion and access in this biggest ever anti-poverty programme is of critical importance for the poor. The chapter discusses how social mobilization by CSOs enables the poor in accessing policy. It illustrates how NREGA impacts on their livelihood and lives when small and marginal farmers as well as women get access to the benefits.

Chapter 4 discusses the potential and limit of social struggles within the space of participatory governance institutions. The chapter examines the case in Sabarkantha District of Gujarat to reveal structural politics that deter the agenda of social justice even as developmental goods and services are accessed. The case shows that as a result of mobilization, there has been a widening of social space and there have been symbolic gains for Dalits. However, the institutions prioritize economic development agenda over the agenda of social justice. Besides, the institutions themselves remain closed to substantial inclusion of Dalit members. This reveals the paradoxes of development and democracy within the local governance institutions of panchayat.

Chapter 5 discusses the dynamics of people's participation in the Joint Forest Management (JFM) Programme in Uttarakhand. Village Forest Committees (VFCs) served as institutional spaces for participation in planning, decision-making and implementation of the programme. The JFM unravels many facets of participation for the poor and socially marginalized. They show that such institutional spaces provide necessary but not sufficient conditions to ensure the democratization of participation in forest management.

Chapter 6 discusses tribal mobilization for land rights led by a grassroots organization in the backward region of Bundelkhand in Uttar Pradesh. The land rights were part of land reforms legislations designed to bring economic development and social justice to the poor. The rights were subverted by the landed and upper castes in collusion with the state administration. The case demonstrates that for the poor and socially vulnerable, economic development and social justice are deeply connected.

Chapter 7 describes the collective economies of the poor built through collective agency and by pooling in collective resources. The economies are based on the ecological resources of land, water and forests that the poor and resourceless people, whom the growth economy has bypassed and who survive on the margins of formal market economy, create for their livelihoods. The economies are collective in ownership, management and distribution of benefits. The collective economies not only practice the ethics of equity, they also practice the sustainable use of ecological resources.

Chapter 8, the last and concluding chapter, reflects on the key issues emerging from the chapters and summarizes them around the theme of democratization of development.

References

Agarwal, A. 1985. 'Ecological Destruction and the Emerging Patterns of Poverty and People's Protest in Rural India'. *Social Action* 35 (1): 54–80.

Bandopadhyay, J., and Shiva, V. 1988. 'Political Economy of Ecology Movements'. *Economic & Political Weekly* 23 (24): 1223–32.

Bardhan, P. 1984. *The Political Economy of Development in India.* Delhi: Oxford University Press.

———. 1988. 'Dominant Proprietary Classes and India's Democracy'. In *India's Democracy: An Analysis of Changing*

State–Society Relation, edited by A. Kohli. Princeton, NJ: Princeton University Press.

Bhatt, C. P. 1991. 'Chipko Movement: The Hug that Saves'. *Survey of the Environment,* 17–19. Madras: The Hindu.

Chandhoke, N. 2005. 'Seeing the State in India'. *Economic & Political Weekly,* 12 March, 40 (11): 1033–39.

Corbridge, S., Williams, G., Srivastava, M., and Veron, R. 2005. *Seeing the State: Governance and Governmentality in India.* Cambridge: Cambridge University Press.

Dhanagre, D. N. 1987. 'Green Revolution and Social Inequalities in Rural India'. *Economic & Political Weekly,* 22 (19, 20 and 21).

Escobar, A. 1995. *Encountering Development: The Making and Unmaking of the Third World.* Princeton, NJ: Princeton University Press.

Esteva, G., and Prakash, M. S. 1999. *Grassroots Postmodernism.* London: Zed Books.

Ferguson, J. 1990. *The Anti-politics Machine: 'Development', Depoliticization and Bureaucratic Power in Lesotho.* Cambridge: Cambridge University Press.

Gibson-Graham, J. K. 2006. *A Postcapitalist Politics.* Minneapolis, MN: University of Minnesota Press.

Gupta, A. 2001. 'Governing Population: The Integrated Child Development Services Program in India'. In *States of Imagination: Ethnographic Explorations of the Postcolonial State,* edited by T. M. Hansen and F. Stepputat. Durham, NC: Duke University Press.

Hansen, T. M., and Stepputat, F., eds. 2001. *States of Imagination: Ethnographic Explorations of the Postcolonial State.* Durham, NC: Duke University Press.

Kohli, A. 1987. *The State and Poverty in India: The Politics of Reform.* Cambridge: Cambridge University Press.

———, ed. 1988. *India's Democracy: An Analysis of Changing State–Society Relation.* Princeton, NJ: Princeton University Press.

Kothari, R. 1986. 'Masses, Classes and the State'. *Economic & Political Weekly,* 21 (5): 210–16.

Mohanty, R. 2014. 'Mobilizing for Democracy: Civil Society Mediation and Access to Policy in India'. In *Mediating States and Citizens: Representing the Marginalized in the Global South,* edited by L. Piper and B. Von Liere. London: Palgrave Macmillan.

Nandy, A. 2003. *The Romance of the State and the Fate of Dissent in the Tropics*. Delhi: Oxford University Press.

Sachs, W. 1997. 'The Need for Home Perspective'. In *The Post-development Reader*, edited by M. Rehnema and V. Bawtree. London: Zed Books.

Shanin, T. 1997. 'The Idea of Progress'. In *The Post-development Reader*, edited by M. Rehnema and V. Bawtree. London: Zed Books.

Tandon, R. 2002. *Participatory Research: Revisiting the Roots*. Delhi: Mosaic.

Truman, H. S. 1949. Available at https://www.trumanlibrary.org/whistlestop/50yr_archive/inagural20jan1949.htm

2

Contesting Development, Reimagining Democracy

Grassroots Social Movements

It has been more than four decades since grassroots-based social movements began contesting the development project of economic growth that lays a heavy emphasis on industrialization and includes, among others, dams, mining, thermal power industries, commercial fishery and forestry. The movements have articulated the ecological and economic consequences for poor people surviving on natural resources of land, water and forest, the resources which development wants to divert into industrial and commercial use.[1] Transcending the limited

---

[1] These aspects of the movements are well documented (Agarwal 1985; Baviskar 1995; Bhatt 1991; Fernandes 1991; Gadgil and Guha 1994; Guha 1989, 1991; Mohanty 2003; Omvedt 1993; Pathak 1994).

critique of specific development projects, the movements critique 'development' with its attendant rationality of technocratic growth, its binary construction of the world into poor and rich, its faith in the linear progress of people and countries from poor/backward/undeveloped to rich/progressive/developed and the unquestioned desirability of this progress.[2] The movements instead urge that the ecology and economy of the poor, with their knowledge and culture, constitute the basis for the reorganization of society, economy and culture (Escobar 1995; Esteva and Prakash 1999; Shiva 1989). Under neoliberalism, the ruthlessness with which economic growth is pursued has led the movements to intensify the protest. People whose interest the movements articulate and represent include the rural poor, small and marginal peasants, landless labourers, people engaged in off-farm activities such as fishermen, and those who earn their livelihood by providing their services to the village such as carpenters, artisans and weavers. In terms of their social composition, the movement members include lower castes, women and tribal communities inhabiting in forests.[3]

[2] That is, the movements no longer believe in finding different or better ways of 'doing development'; they critique and reject the entire paradigm of development. This has led to the shift from alternative development to alternative to development (Escobar 1995).

[3] When livelihood resources such as lands, rivers, lakes and forests are threatened by development, we find that affluent people—affluent peasants in the case of Narmada dam which threatens to submerge the agricultural land and habitat of hundreds of villages, and affluent fishermen as in case of the Tata Company's commercial prawn cultivation project in the Chilika Lake which threatened the interests of fishermen, rich and poor alike—are also part of the same movement. This has led the movements face the critical question as to whose interest they represent. A subaltern approach to movement politics (Guha 1982), I suggest, will help understand this. The movements are the domain of the poor and marginalized. In spite of the involvement of the affluent and locally dominant groups in social movements, the movements are not in response to their needs, and as long as they subscribe to and take part in the core politics of the movement which represent the interests of the poor and marginalized, they are part of the same social action, and their membership in the movement is no reason to discredit the discourse of the movement.

The history of these grassroots movements reveals their power to shape the discourse of development to make it democratic in its form, practice and outcome. In this sense, 'development' questions become questions about democracy. I argue in this chapter that the contestations over development are also contestations over democratic politics, for they raise the questions of equity, equality and inclusion. The movements have led to the re-surfacing of the old questions of democratic distribution of material benefits of development back to the surface and also infused them with new meanings by emphasizing the democratic principles and practices that development has undermined. The movements have filled the spaces left vacant in a formal democracy where neither the local governance spaces created by the state for participation nor the political parties have represented the interests of the poor and the marginalized. The movements have thus rejected these spaces and emerged as depoliticized sites of alternative grassroots democratic politics. As such, the resistance movements can be looked as acts of deepening of democracy.

This chapter discusses how grassroots movements democratize development. The chapter does so by elaborating what I call 'deepening democracy tasks' that the movements have come to perform in recent times. The movements perform following five such deepening democracy tasks:

- The movements replace the exclusionary narrative of state-led development with a counter-narrative of inclusion.
- The movements expand the non-party political spaces for social action.
- Public space is constantly being democratized by the movements.
- The movements re-negotiate poor people's relationship with the state.
- The movements are sites of reconstruction of modernity through the discourse of citizenship and rights.

The Trajectory of Economic Growth

Economic growth through industrialization and commodity production has remained the core of Indian economy ever since India embarked upon the path of planned development. There are many streams of industrial development. One stream generates raw material for industrial use, for example, mining and steel industries. The power projects are designed to generate power for industrial, agriculture and domestic consumption—dams and thermal power plants come under this category. Another stream uses technology to harness natural resources such as marine resources and fisheries for export promotion, and yet another stream captures the natural resources, primarily forests, for commercial use such as paper, textile industries, etc. Industrialization thus uses nature as its primary raw material to generate material wealth. Mega dams, such as Mayurakshi, Nagarjuna Sagar and Hirakud, NTPC and steel industries in Bhilai, Rourkela and Jamshedpur became the hallmarks of growth in the first phase of industrial growth. Since the beginning of industrialization, the public sector controlled the industrial development with a peripheral role assigned to the private sector in light consumer goods. This changed when India liberalized the economy and ushered in globalization. The private sector, including foreign capital, made an entry into the rural areas.

India entered its second phase of growth in the 1990s. The liberalization reforms facilitated the investment of private capital including foreign capital. A new industrial policy was formulated in 1991 to facilitate industrial growth. Growth centres[4] and SEZs[5] were created to pursue the neoliberal growth. This

[4] The provinces demarcated geographical locations as growth centres to develop them as industrial hubs with special investment of resources.

[5] The creation of SEZs for export promotion, setting up of industry and infrastructure development is facilitated by the SEZ Act 2005, under which the SEZs enjoy duty-free import/domestic procurement of goods, operation and maintenance of SEZ units. SEZs also enjoy 100%

resulted in rapid economic growth among which industry and SEZs feature prominently. The new environment gave rise to competition among provinces to behave 'investment friendly' and added to their zeal to allow the uncritical entry of private industries.

With the growth of private and global capital, the role of the state has shrunk. The retreat of the state under neoliberalism and its changing role to mere facilitator also means that the state, while still doing the midwifery role for industrial growth, has lost much of its power to deliver vis-à-vis its citizens. It is not merely the question of redistribution of benefits of industrialization; it is also the normative role the state is expected to play in protecting the rights of its citizens. Under neoliberalism, both have suffered.

A striking feature of industrialization under the neoliberal phase has been the aggressiveness with which it is pursued. On 16 December 2006, three people were killed in a police firing in Maikanch village, Kashipur, Odisha, when the police took to extremes of violence to suppress the local resistance to UAIL.[6] On 2 January 2006, the police fired at the people protesting against the Tata Steel SEZ in Kalinganagar, Odisha, killing 12 tribal people. On 14 March 2007, the state retaliated to people's protest against the proposed SEZ for Salim Group of Chemicals in Nandigram, West Bengal, and 13 people were killed by the police. Nandigram, since then, turned into a site

Income Tax exemption on export income for the SEZ units for the first five years and 50% for the next five years. Ministry of Commerce and Industry web portal on SEZ (http://sezindia.nic.in) gives rationale of the SEZs and the incentives given to them. However, SEZs in many parts of India have given rise to conflicts between industry and government standing on one side and the local populace on the other due to forceful acquisition of productive agricultural land from farmers (*Frontline* 2006).

[6] UAIL was a consortium of industries from India (Hindalco and Tata), Canada (ALCAN) and Norway (Norsk Hydro). Tata, Norsk Hydro and ALCAN withdrew due to local resistance.

of the worst kind of violence where the Left party-ruled state administration had launched a planned operation in which its cadre-based men and police stormed the Nandigram villages to capture them with force.[7] The terror the state perpetrated in recent times as exemplified by the brutal killings of poor people in Kashipur, Kalinganagar and Nandigram reveals not only the ugly side of development under neoliberalism but also the extent the state can go to pursue it even if it means curtailing the most fundamental rights of people, that is, the right to life.[8] Development as public good has not only remained a long forgotten rhetoric, but the situation has worsened for the poor who cannot interrogate the state and the industry primarily because they have remained far too long at the far end of the boons of the economy.

Development and Discontent

In the history of industrialization in India, the social contract has remained between the state and people. Even when private investments have played a larger role as industrial capital, the state still takes the responsibility for impact assessments, social and environmental clearance, land acquisition for projects and resettlement of people displaced by such projects. Even as a facilitator of industrialization, the state's role is critical.

National growth as public good has remained the most persuasive and legitimizing claim of the state for acquiring land for industrialization. Nehru evoked the sentiment when he said to the people whose lands were taken by the Hirakud Dam, 'If you are to suffer, you should suffer in the interest of the nation'. Land Acquisition Act, 1894, a piece of colonial administration that vested immense power in the hands of the state, was used

---

[7] The citizen report on Nandigram gives a vivid account of the brutal events that took place in the Nandigram villages during October–November 2007 (Sanhati n.d.).

[8] Following the Gandhian tradition, the movements have been largely peaceful.

unsparingly to acquire both private and public land. The Land Acquisition Act was revised in 2013 and renamed as The Right to Fair Compensation and Transparency in Land Acquisition Rehabilitation and Resettlement Act, 2013. The Act provides for the resettlement of all affected people. It does not, however, have compensation for land acquired unless the displaced family/person has legal title to the land. The Act sidesteps the prohibition on tribal land being transferred to non-tribals by allowing acquisition for private companies or for public–private partnership projects. The 2014 ordinance which amends the 2013 Act replaces 'private company' with 'private entity'.

Tribal land is one of the most contentious issues in land acquisition (Mohanty 2007). The rights of the tribals on their land is inalienable, that is, the land belonging to tribal people cannot be transferred to non-tribals, and any such transfer has to be ratified by the gram sabha and panchayat. Tribal lands, including rights on private as well as common property, are governed by two legislations—Panchayat Extension to Schedule Area Act, 1996, and Scheduled Tribes and Other Traditional Forest Dwellers (Recognition of Forest Rights) Act, 2006. Both the Acts vest power in the gram sabha and panchayat. Despite legal safeguards, the tribal rights over their land have been usurped for industries, particularly mining, as the tribal areas are repository of mineral wealth. The mining rich states such as Odisha, Jharkhand and Chhattisgarh are heavily populated by tribal people. The local resistance to mining is thus gaining momentum in tribal areas.

The Vedanta mining in Odisha which is facing stiff resistance represents the schism between people and the company. In 2003, Vedanta Aluminium Limited (VAL), a subsidiary of Vedanta Resources, signed a memorandum of understanding with the Government of Odisha to set up an alumina refinery plant and to conduct bauxite mining. Both the refinery and mining are carried out in forest regions inhabited by tribals. The project has run into controversies and is facing the wrath of the local people, the Dongria Kondh, a tribal community that has been living for generations in the Niyamgiri Hills, where Vedanta has proposed mining. While the land for the refinery has already been obtained, the protest has escalated to stop the mining.

Niyamgiri mountains, which VAL wants to acquire for mining, has been inhabited by the 8,000 strong Dongria Kondh tribe for generations living in harmony with nature. Niyamgiri is also the abode of their deity, Niyam. The bauxite reserves at the top of the hills act as a sponge that soaks up the monsoon rains and then holds water during summer. Due to this reserve, there are perennial streams in the mountain. The Dongrias thus see mining as dangerous; it would displace them from their habitat, destroy their livelihood and pollute the environment.

Vedanta submitted an application in 2004 to the Ministry of Environment and Forest for the reallocation of forest land. The clearance for the refinery was given followed by a clearance for mining in 2008. The protest escalated following the clearance. During the second stage of clearance for the project, the Supreme Court intervened, and for the first time in India an environmental referendum was held in 12 villages in 2013. The gram sabha in all the villages, where the referendum was held, rejected the mining project. The Vedanta, however, did not withdraw.

Displacement of the poor from their habitat and livelihood has been the most critical fall out of growth and has added additional disadvantages to their already disadvantaged position. As the techno-centric economic growth took off and huge irrigation, hydel projects and heavy industries took shape, thousands of people were displaced from their original habitat. Without adequate resettlement and rehabilitation, displacement became the inevitable fate of people ousted by development projects (Baboo 1991; Fernandes 2007; Mohapatra 1991). During the early phase of industrialization, resettlement was provided in the form of cash compensation for the land acquired. Later, land compensation was added as a resettlement offer.

There are many caveats and shortcomings in the way resettlement and rehabilitation have taken shape. There is seldom any prior information or discussion with people regarding acquisition of their land. Cash compensation is never adequate for what people lose as their livelihood and habitat. Land for land, though sounds good, has faced immense difficulty as availability of good quality land and closer to where people have lived all their lives has remained a challenge. Besides, those who do not have legal rights to their land such as tenants or children in undivided Hindu households do not get land compensation. In the case of Sardar Sarovar Dam displacement, land for land was offered as compensation for the first time. The displaced people from Madhya Pradesh were provided land in Maharashtra. The land provided was of poor quality and non-irrigable, and the land titles were not provided even when people lost their land and moved to the new location. In many cases, the host community was hostile to the new settlers. Even though housing was provided, people were made to live in temporary arrangements, sometimes under tin shades, for a long period (TISS n.d.).

As a compensation for the loss of livelihood, the projects often promise job to people. This promise, however, is seldom formalized through a contract between the project and the communities. The jobs in which people are absorbed are invariably unskilled or at best semi-skilled in nature, and they are available mostly during the construction phase of a project. There are instances where the companies bring outside labour as they fear trouble from local people (Ranga Rao and Kumar 2003).

The growth projects also affect people in indirect ways. Pollution of agricultural land and water bodies due to industrial effluents have caused people to abandon cultivation and move to other places. Industrial dust in mining areas affects the health of local residents. Women, old people and children become most vulnerable to displacement. The sum total is that while people lose their livelihood resources, and are ousted from their habitat, what they encounter is not only the lack of interest and indifference on the part of the government to address their situation but also aggression and physical violence against them.

The sacrifice the poor have to make for the national interest remains an unchallenged idea as much as the idea that the trickle-down effect would eventually benefit them.

The people who were once at the forefront of the resistance in Kalinganagar SEZ have become quiet after 12 people were killed.

When Neelachal Ispat[9] began in the early 1970s, we had believed it would create the second *ispat nagar* (steel city) on the model of Rourkela. But that did not happen. There are no jobs for us here. That exposed the myth of industrialization. It needs our land but what does it gives us back in return? (personal communication with tribal people in Kalinganagar)

The Birth of People's Movement

For almost two decades, there was acceptance of industrialization as a strategy of national growth, but, during the 1970s, voices began to be raised against it. The resistance movements articulated three issues: national growth and public good had turned into private good benefiting only a section of the population, that is, the elites in a position to negotiate with the state; the natural resources of land, river and forest on which rural communities were dependent for survival were taken away for development without providing them with alternative means of survival; and decision-making about development had been centralized, denying poor people the chance to voice their opinion. The democratic agenda of development was at a crisis.

The Chipko Movement, which heralded people's resistance to the loss of forests, was a movement by the local people, particularly women, in the hills of Garhwal in Western Himalayas to save their forest from commercial felling. It was initiated

[9] Refers to the Neelachal Ispat Nigam Limited—a public sector steel industry.

in the early 1970s, a period significant for the Stockholm Conference on Environment. Chipko Movement brought home the truth that environmental degradation and social inequalities are intrinsically linked (Bhatt 1991; Guha 1991). The success of the movement was followed by resistance against big dams, mines, commercial fisheries and forestry and industrial pollution in many parts of the country. The movements have intensified the resistance in the post-liberalized era.

This chapter will not enter deeper into the now well-known school of new social movements to examine in detail whether the movements discussed here indeed represent the new social movements which emerged in Europe, where a new post-industrial political consciousness (as opposed to the old class-based struggles of industrial society) helped shaping new identities and new concerns for ecology, peace, feminism and civil rights (Melucci 1995; Offe 1985; Touraine 1985). A brief theoretical positioning, however, will help situate the movements in India and in the developing countries.

When the grassroots movements in India began protesting against state-led development in the early 1970s, there were considerable debates whether the movements were indeed new forms of protest or were continuations of the old struggles of poor people for equity, albeit in a new form. Both academic and popular writing claimed that while the movements were reflective of a new consciousness about ecology, they were also fundamentally old struggles by the poor for control over ecology-based livelihood resources (Agarwal 1985; Guha 1989, 1991). Old struggles in this context did not always signify quintessential class-based struggles in an industrial society; instead, the movements covered a wide range, from protest movements during the colonial period waged against the kings and the British rulers to agrarian movements pitched by the peasants against the landowners after India gained independence. In fact, the articulation of contemporary movements as struggles against poverty and inequality that emanate from the commercial use of ecological resources on which poor people subsist helped establish the link between ecological consequences of development and poverty in the developing countries, thus giving a wider and new connotation to such movements.

This new perspective of the movements also expanded the framework of the 'identity' politics of the European new social movements, whose membership cut across class and profession in registering protest against ecological degradation. The movements in India have illustrated that the identities that movements mobilize to contest development comprise both old identities of caste, class and gender and new identities such as dam-displaced or project-affected. Since the poor, lower castes, tribal people and women invariably become victims of large-scale development projects, the movements' construct of identities cuts across a number of particular identities and provides a mix of old and new.

Seen in the context of earlier movements, however, the movements which have animated the terrain of grassroots protest since the 1970s appear new in three significant ways: the movements have linked ecology-based livelihood struggles with the large-scale development the state follows; the movements have targeted 'development' and the state, and not any particular group of dominant people; and the movements have kept away from party political affiliation and have emerged as de-political sites to represent the interests of the poor.

The Deepening Democracy Tasks the Movements Perform

Replacing the Exclusionary Narratives of Development with a Counter-narrative of Inclusion

In their acts of contestation over development, movement actors associate three sets of meanings to the consequences of development: a material meaning that talks about the loss of livelihood resources and consequent impoverishment of the poor; a social meaning that talks about the disruption of community relationships of those displaced by development; and a political meaning that talks about the non-consultative, top-down, imposing nature of decision-making around development. Running through the three sets of meanings is the feeling of exclusion—from the material benefits of development, from the social and cultural connections and from political decision-making. The counter-narrative the movement gives rise to, therefore, is inclusion of the marginalized sections—poor, lower castes, women and tribals—both in the processes and outcomes of development.

As large-scale development takes away the sustenance resources of land, water and forest from the communities that have been subsisting on them, the concerns of livelihood and resultant poverty loom as questions that are at once about equity and ecology. Chipko Movement was the first of its kind, which drew the connection between livelihood, equity of resource distribution and consideration for the ecological resources of the poor. Gradually, other aspects of livelihood became more visible and began to be articulated by the movements that came up against mining, dams, chemical industries and commercial fisheries. The large-scale displacement of people by dams, mines and industries became synonymous with development. Without any adequate policy to resettle the displaced population, loss of livelihood and habitat, migration to cities, consequent transformation of peasants into wage labour in the cities where they finally end up living as illegal inhabitants in the slums became the ugly faces of development. Even in those instances when the industries did not displace people, the pollution of agricultural land and water resources caused by mines, fisheries and chemical industries meant loss of livelihood for people.

The material aspects of displacement, loss of livelihood and migration are intricately connected with the disruption of socio-cultural contexts and communitarian relations. Not only did displaced people lose old relationships but also the resentment of the host communities the displaced people became subjected to in the new settings intensified their feeling of alienation. The competition for scarce resources of drinking water, agricultural land, village common, etc., became sources of conflict. Even in instances where the project tried to resettle few families, the transition from one's own place to the other generated a feeling of loss. The temporary shelter that was built for the resettled people, the uncertainty about the possession of the land allotted to them, the attitude of charity and harassment they faced in the government offices dealing with the resettlement and finally the aggression shown by the old inhabitants where the new resettlement colonies were built all meant the loss of certainty and comfort of their social relationships built over generations. In many instances, displaced people migrated to the cities in search of livelihood only to be turned to wage workers from farmers, and live in the squalor of urban slums.

At the heart of material and social exclusion lies the exclusion from political decision-making. Industrial development under the rubric of national and public good never allowed poor people to voice their opinion in the design and implementation of projects. Often people came to know about a project when government officials came to acquire their land.

The three dimensions of exclusion resulting from development are articulated by the movement actors as the dominant narrative of development, which is about the lack of distributive logic of material benefits of development, its cultural insensitivity and its centralization of decision-making. The contestation of *exclusionary* narratives of development with a counter-narrative of the *inclusion* of the marginalized groups, therefore, entails not only democratization of the *outcomes* of development but also, equally important, democratization of the *processes* of development. The powerlessness and exclusion that emanate from not being able to counter or tame development on their own terms gets a double dose of defeat due to the aspirations people have from a democratic polity of which they form a part. The mobilizations contesting development, therefore, are articulation of interests that resonates with the democratic ethos of inclusion and equality.

The movements do not only see an insertion of the principles of inclusion in the existing framework of development as their goal but also envisioning a new framework whose foundation is laid on the principles of inclusion and whose outcomes are measured on the basis of equality, equity and social justice. This, the movements argue, demands not only an alternative to development but also an alternative democratic politics as articulated by the poor people through their acts of protests.

Expansion of Non-party Political Space for Social Action

The 1970s were the period when, for the first time in Indian history since independence, acts of resistance began reflecting disenchantment with the political parties as representatives of interest of the marginalized groups. Until then the Congress, as the main vehicle of the nationalist struggle and subsequently as the ruling party, enjoyed unquestionable faith bestowed on it to fulfil the aspirations of people. But after two decades of rule, Congress was seen as the party of the elites and dominant interest—rural and industrial bourgeoisie and upper castes. The Left then became the vanguard of worker and peasant movements. The voices of dissent from students, women, peasants and labour soon discarded party affiliations and, instead of targeting the class enemy in the quintessential manner of the Left, began directing against the state for the failed aspirations, demanding its responsiveness.

This was a period when development began to be resisted in a very different manner. Chipko Movement was the continuation of the old peasant struggle, but it added new dimensions to the struggle by raising the issue of survival, dependence and control of the people over their resources and by directing the struggle not against any class per se but against the state (Guha 1991). Jayaprakash Narayan with his Sampoorn Kranti (total revolution) to restructure the entire economy, polity and society captured national imagination in a way that was second only to the nationalist movement. Kothari (1984) calls these protests without political party affiliations as 'non-party political formations', which declared the autonomy of social actions from political parties.

A series of events unfolded on the political landscape that demonstrated the limited ability of the political parties to articulate the ordinary people's interest in a meaningful way. The imposition of National Emergency by the Congress under Indira Gandhi in 1975 to suppress the voices of dissent, the electoral loss of Congress in the election when emergency was lifted, victory of the Janata Party and subsequent crisis in the party for the post of prime minister, leading eventually to putting Congress back in power were some of the key events of the 1970s. This signalled the crisis of a representative democracy to articulate the interests of the poor and marginalized and gave rise to autonomous social actors, who carved out a space for action uncontaminated by formal politics where they could raise their voice and interests.

The crisis of representative democracy has deepened under neoliberalism. Because neoliberalism offers 'development' as a new source for political legitimacy, both the ruling and opposition parties in India have clung to it to create their constituencies. If the ruling parties have clung to 'development' to invite foreign investment and create an 'investor friendly' image for themselves, with the long-term interest to stay in power by catering to the interest of the industry and global capital, the opposition has clung to it to create a pro-poor anti-development image.

In a historical irony, on 14 March 2007, the Left-led government of West Bengal opened fire on people who had assembled at Nandigram to protest against the acquisition of their land for the SEZ. In the events that unfolded in Nandigram during October and November 2007, the Left front workers together with the police captured the site of protest and kept the movement's sympathizers and the press out of the site. When tribal people were killed by the police in Kashipur in December 2006 and Kalinganagar in January 2006, the ruling government in

Odisha was led by Biju Janata Dal, an alliance of right wing Bharatiya Janata Party. The Congress, as the party in opposition in the Odisha government, rushed to sympathize with the protesters. But that act was highly suspicious as the Congress as the ruling party at the national level was at the helm of facilitating neoliberal reforms, economic policy and planning. In the same state in the early 1990s, the Congress, then in power sanctioned an intensive prawn cultivation project by the Tata, not caring for the livelihood of the poor fishermen (Mohanty 2003).

In such contexts, the movements, being non-party political formations, help create autonomy for the social actors protesting development without any party allegiance. The movements also help in extending the civil society space, which is vital for democracy and which remained subsumed under the state during the first two decades of independence. If, as Mouffe (2000) says, democracy itself is constituted of interests that it cannot rise above but can at best manage and balance, then we have to seek that counter-balancing force in civil society. It has to stay separable from the state, remain visible and articulate interests of those whom the state, even a democratic one, neglects in many instances. The movements exist not to capture the state power, but curbing that power and making the state respond to its neglected citizenry. In the absence of civil society, state can be pervasive, and, even if it demonstrates its capacity for development, it can curtail people's freedom to choose development on their own terms. This space is significant for transforming what Habermas (1989) calls 'political public' to engage in 'politics' without a political party affiliation.

Democratization of Public Space

As representative of public good, movements are acts of the creation of public spaces which are democratic in nature and content. Besides creating autonomous public spaces that are non-political in nature, movements also work towards democratizing the public space by saving them from being hijacked and invaded by vested powers. The expansion of public spaces based on the principles of equality, rights and citizenship is what Melucci calls a process of 'post-industrial democratization'.

> [The public spaces enable] movements to articulate the demands of civil society and to render the power relations of complex societies more visible. Given that power in these systems tends to conceal itself behind a veil of allegedly neutral or technical decision-making procedures, this critical function of public space is indispensable and probably of primary importance in the present period. (Melucci 1989, 230)

The idea of public spheres gained currency in the work of Habermas, who sees it as a site for deliberation and communicative action. Arguments and reason, not status, are what Habermas demarcates as the defining principles of public sphere. As a site for equality and freedom, public spaces are sites for empowerment and political modernity (Habermas 1989). Public sphere which is not pervaded by the state and where individuals can deliberate to create a rational public will is thus vital for democracy and citizen participation. Writing in the context of Western Europe, Habermas was quite aware that the public sphere could be a bourgeoisie sphere governed by possession of property and education and, in that sense, antithetical to the democratic ideas of equality. Hence, he contended that the public sphere has to accommodate common people, their will and universal possibilities. As he puts it, 'The public sphere of civil society stood or fell with the principle of universal access. A public sphere from which specific groups would be *eo ipso* excluded was less than merely incomplete; it was not a public sphere at all' (Habermas 1989, 85).

Despite its being conceptualized as 'public', there is nothing inherent in public space that prevents it from getting captured and co-opted by dominant interests, official discourses and manipulative truths. In a hierarchical society such as India, divided along multiple lines, public spaces can be hijacked by powerful interests. Writing about the public consultation processes of NTPC, a public sector enterprise located in Andhra

Pradesh, on the issues of resettlement, Newell (2006) remarks that the industry often manipulates the practice in such a way that keeps the actual stakeholders outside the public hearing. The industry is required to put the date and place of consultation in a newspaper prior to the meeting so that people are informed about the process and can join it. It often puts the information in English newspapers and not in vernacular ones, however, and does so only a few days prior to the event, so that either people don't read about the meeting or, even when few of them get to know about it, the time is too short for them to attend. Public spaces are also susceptible to be invaded by the powerful. As the Nandigram incident showed, public spaces can be invaded to silence the voice of protest. When the ruling government invaded Nandigram and the police fired at the protestors, Buddhadeb Bhattacharya, the then chief minister of West Bengal, referred to his retaliation against the Bhumi Uchhed Pratirodh Committee (Committee against Land Evictions), the organization spearheading the protest, as 'paying back in the same coin' (Mahapatra 2007).

Hence, efforts to expand the public space to accommodate the opinion and interests of the powerless, to keep it open to debates and deliberations that are not contaminated by political and official interests and to safeguard the public spaces so as not to let them be captured by the powerful are critical for deepening of democracy. Movements perform this critical task of expanding and safeguarding the public spaces as sites of alternative democratic politics that is different from the state and other vested interests.

Renegotiation of Relationship with the State

The movements embody the conceptualizations and practices of deprived groups focused on reformulating their relationship with the state. In India, development, as pointed out earlier, was intended to operate within the democratic framework. Development gradually became the overarching domain, however, eclipsing democratic practices. The first two decades after independence witnessed absolute faith in state and its agenda of 'nation-building', that is, reconstruction of a post-colonial society. Nation-building legitimized both development, and the state as its designer and executer. Faith on the rationality and neutrality of both development and the state was absolute, unquestioning and without suspicion. As Chandhoke (1998, 32) puts it,

> Development was considered to be a value-free social process and a desirable end. That it could breed its own pattern of social oppression was neither recognized nor appreciated... narrowly conceived in an econometric fashion, development portrayed the state as an impersonal vehicle of social change. It not only ejected the power relations of the state from its discourse, it also excluded the power relations implicit in the model of development itself. The underlying assumption was that the state could develop its people and hence should be the repository of untrammelled power.

Ironically, while power was kept out of the rhetoric of development, development became the space not only for strengthening old forms of division and inequality based on class, ethnicity and gender, but it also created new forms of inequality as large number of people displaced by industrial development became impoverished, migrated to other places as labourers or ended up as unskilled workers in urban industrial towns. Here the state, as the chief force propelling development, was seen as an authoritarian agency of power and imposition with which people could not relate. It is of little surprise, then, that development was seized on by the powerless groups to contest inequalities and that the state was kept at the centre of this rebellion and reform. The movements do not aim to abrogate state power or to achieve a stateless utopia; they aim to reformulate the relationship between the state and its neglected citizenry within a democratic ethos, howsoever contentious that may appear.

The agenda of this reformulation of relationship with the state is not straightforward; it is fraught with complexities. For one, the state, as several incidents have demonstrated, has used force to silence the voices of dissent. This is particularly evident during rallies and demonstrations, which are seen as challenging the state in public. The Narmada Movement against the Sardar Sarovar Project, the Chilika Movement against the prawn cultivation project of the corporate house of Tata, the movement against the Subarnarekha Dam, the movement against the UAIL project and, in recent times, movements against SEZs have all witnessed police atrocities.

Second, the state has shown its preference for a certain kind of relationship with the groups working for the marginalized sections. Agragamee, the organization that once spearheaded the movement against the aluminium mining by the multinationals in the Kashipur region of Odisha, having enjoyed a good relationship with the state for its pioneering work on food security, faced its wrath for 'anti-government activities'. In other words, as long as the organization worked for the livelihood of the poor tribal communities without questioning the state, it was not seen as a threat; in fact, it was seen as 'behaving like the state' in taking care of needy people. These acts indicate that the state still retains the upper hand in shaping the state–society relationship.

There is also evidence to the contrary, however, of the state succumbing to people's demands,[10] although such instances are rare. In the recent times, the judiciary, unlike the legislative and executive arms of the state, have shown sympathy with the movements. The repeated stay orders from Supreme Court on the construction of the Sardar Sarovar Dam is an example. These small victories against the state are indications that the state can be tamed, although the process can be arduous.

[10] One such example is the success of the movement against the commercial export-oriented prawn cultivation project—integrated shrimp farming project—of the Tata Company, which threatened the livelihood of fishermen subsisting on the Chilika Lake in Odisha (Mohanty 2003).

The movements as attempts to democratize the relationship of the state with millions of its poor are therefore not to be seen as alternative ideologies of statelessness but as ideologies of reform. This agenda of reform, however, should not be reduced to or conflated with the neoliberal reforms of 'good governance' spearheaded by the Bretton Woods Institutions comprising the World Bank and the International Monetary Fund, which see the state as an ahistorical and apolitical agency and emphasize its administrative efficiency. The social movements, on the contrary, want to bring 'politics' back to the state and infuse its formulation of development with a strategy for negotiation of power and resource by the deprived groups. Writing about contemporary movements, Melucci (1988, 259) says, 'The public spaces which are beginning to develop in complex societies are points of connection between political institutions and collective demands, between the functions of government and the representatives of conflict'.

Reconstruction of Modernity through the Discourses of Citizenship and Rights

In their resistance to development, the movements have sought to counter modernity, which informs development, and reinvent it in their interest by speaking through the language of citizenship and right, that is, through the language of democracy. The contestation of modernity takes place at the global level; it also takes place within the boundaries of the nation state. The global modernity becomes more pervasive under neoliberalism.

There are two ways in which global modernity works. First, the basic foundation of modernity which speaks about the universal agenda of economic growth and rationality of linear progression of human societies based on the dualism of progress from rural to urban, backward to progressive, traditional to modern and poor to rich is reinvented to create a global economy through the invasion of economies of poor countries by the rich and powerful. Second, with neoliberalism, the nation states are brought into the world system in a manner unprecedented in history. Development in many of its aspects, therefore, has now acquired a global connotation, and seems to have slipped out of the grasp of the nation states, which earlier had the authority to decide the nature of development within their boundaries.

Hence, the fact that movements have to contest global modernity, and the coalescing of movements in the global sphere, more prominently in the form of World Social Forum, is indication of the contestation over global modernity. The movements also contest a micro or localized version of modernity, however, within the boundaries of the nation state. The micro-modernity is drawn from macro-modernity but, as the Indian experience suggests, is shaped by yet another form of modernity, which is liberal democracy. As Oommen (2004) writes, 'The very act of framing of development with a democratic discourse, and the state strategies of distributive justice, equality, freedom, all have given rise to expectations from modernity, the failed promises of which have crystallised the construction of the movements'. Rather than denying modernity altogether, however, the movements have tried to reinvent it through the very modern language of citizenship and rights, which talks of both development and its democracy-building agenda. It is as if to take revenge on modernity and its agents— the state, market and their joint product, development. The movements have claimed the language of citizenship and rights to counter modernity on its own terms. By speaking a language that is intelligible to modernity, the movements have invented the weapon with which to contest and reconstruct it.

The movement discourse challenges the liberal notions of universal citizenship located in the constitutional guarantees of rights. The disadvantaged location of the poor and their subjective experiences of oppression and powerlessness have led to the resurfacing of the questions of 'particular' identities, experiences and meanings associated with citizenship (Mohanty and Tandon 2006). As a practice of democracy, these questions, on the one hand, make visible the tenuous assumptions of equality in a liberal democracy and, on the other, make claims of equity and equality for those who have remained at the margins of citizenship.

As mentioned, the identities that movements mobilize to contest development comprise both the old identities of caste, class and gender and the new identities, such as dam-displaced, or project-affected. Since invariably the poor, lower castes, tribal people and women become victims of large-scale development projects, the movements often construct identities that cut across a number of particular identities. For instance 'fishermen' became an identity for mobilization against the struggle in Chilika opposing the Tata Company. The fishermen identity symbolically combined the twin identities of class/occupation and caste. Since fishermen belong to the low caste, are poor and dependent on fishing for their livelihood, invoking the identity of fishermen meant conveying the message that it was a struggle for the assertion of low class/low caste identities. Similarly, in the Narmada Movement, the identities invoked are *adivasi–kisan–mazdoor* (tribal–farmer–labourer). These combine the class identity with tribal identity. Both old and new identities are thus mobilized for claiming citizenship. The old identity shows the continuation of old forms of exploitation; the new identity shows the new contexts of exclusion.

The second aspect that the movements have highlighted through the language of citizenship, is the agency of people in shaping the developmental agenda. The state-invented term 'beneficiary' subjects people to the patronage and dominance of the state, and the market-invented term 'client' talks to limited range of people who can be part of its ever expanding profit-seeking agenda, thus leaving a large number of poor people outside its periphery. But poor people are not beneficiaries or clients; they are autonomous actors whose agency has to be recognized in shaping the society, economy and polity in which they live. Hence, citizens as 'actors' in the scheme of development and governance is what the movements emphasize on.

The language of rights is used by the movement actors to counter the might of the state. If the notion of national and public good gave the state the power to acquire land, forest and river, the communities subsisting on these resources are now claiming their ownership and control over them, giving a different meaning to 'public good'. It is at the very moment of their interface with the state that illiterate communities learn the potential of 'rights' to make their claim. And the claim for rights over subsistence resources have drawn people's attention to many other rights, which were given by the state in the form of various legislations but never actualized. The tribal people in Kashipur in Rayagada District, Odisha, in their opposition to the UAIL, not only invoked the rights of protection of their land, they simultaneously invoked the rights to be free from bonded labour and from money lenders, thus articulating the conditions desirable for a dignified life and living. The tribal people opposing the Vedanta mining in Niyamgiri, Kalahandi District, Odisha, are fighting to save their way of life and their culture even as they fight to save their land. In the context of police repression, the right claim has highlighted the right to life and right to freedom of speech and expression, which constitute the inalienable fundamental rights guaranteed to citizens under the Constitution of India.

The movements are not merely invoking the state-given rights, they are also expanding the scope of the rights by articulating those which are new, which are not given in the Constitution but have grown from the lived experiences of being marginalized and from the struggles waged to address that marginalization, for example, rights over survival resources of land, water and forests, and rights for self-determination about development. As Dagnino (2005, 155) writes:

> In this sense, the very determination of the meaning of rights, and the assertion of something as a right, are themselves objects of political struggle.... Moreover, this redefinition comes to include not only the right to *equality*, but also the right to *difference*, which deepens and broadens the right to equality.

The chapter argued that the acts of resistance to development are also to be understood as acts of deepening of democratic politics as conceptualized by the poor. This is critical in a country such as India, where the development planning by the state began by associating democratic outcomes of equity and equality with development. While that goal of development was soon forgotten by the state, it lingered in people's imagination and thus shaped their expectation. Hence, the questions of development at once become questions of democracy. The movements thus perform critical democracy-deepening tasks as they question development, its attendant rationality and its consequences for the poor, and as they organize people to resist development and its undemocratic enactors—the state, industry and their modernization project.

References

Agarwal, A. 1985. 'Ecological Destruction and the Emerging Patterns of Poverty and People's Protest in Rural India'. *Social Action* 35 (1): 54–80.

Baboo, B. 1991. 'Big Dams and the Tribals: The Case of the Hirakud Dam Oustees'. *Social Action* 41 (3): 288–303.

Bardhan, P. 1984. *The Political Economy of Development in India*. Delhi: Oxford University Press.

———. 1988. 'Dominant Proprietary Classes and India's Democracy'. In *India's Democracy: An Analysis of Changing State–Society Relation*, edited by A. Kohli. Princeton, NJ: Princeton University Press.

Baviskar, A. 1995. *In the Belly of the River: Tribal Conflicts Over Development in the Narmada Valley*. Delhi: Oxford University Press.

Bhatt, C. P. 1991. 'Chipko Movement: The Hug that Saves'. *Survey of the Environment, The Hindu*, 17–23.

Chandhoke. N. 1998. 'The Assertion of Civil Society Against the State: The Case of Post-Colonial World'. In *People's Rights: Social Movements and the State in the Third World*, edited by M. Mohanty, P. N. Mukherjee, and O. Törnquist. New Delhi: SAGE.

Dagnino, E. 2005. 'We All Have Rights but... Contesting Concepts of Citizenship in Brazil'. In *Inclusive Citizenship*, edited by N. Kabeer. London: Zed Books.

Dhanagre, D. N. 1987. 'Green Revolution and Social Inequalities in Rural India'. *Economic & Political Weekly* 22: AN137–44.

Escobar, A. 1995. *Encountering Development: The Making and Unmaking of the Third World*. Princeton, NJ: Princeton University Press.

Esteva, G., and Prakash, M. S. 1999. *Grassroots Postmodernism*. London: Zed Books.

Fernandes, W. 1991. 'Power and Powerlessness: Development Projects and Displacement of Tribals'. *Social Action* 41 (3): 243–70.

———. 2007. 'Singur and the Displacement Scenario'. *Economic & Political Weekly*, 42 (3): 203–06.

Frontline. 2006. 'Rural Resistance'. *Frontline* 23 (20): 7–20.

Gadgil, M., and Guha, R. 1994. 'Ecological Conflicts and the Environmental Movement in India'. *Development and Change* 25 (1): 101–36.

Guha, R. 1982. 'On Some Aspects of the Historiography of Colonial India'. In *Subaltern Studies I: Writings on South Asian History and Society*, edited by R. Guha. Delhi: Oxford University Press.

———. 1989. 'New Social Movements: The Problem'. *Seminar* No. 355, March.

———. 1991. *The Unquiet Woods: Ecological Change and Peasant Resistance in the Himalaya*. Delhi: Oxford University Press.

Habermas, J. 1989. *The Structure of the Public Sphere*. Cambridge: Polity Press.

Hansen, T. B., and Stepputat, F., eds. 2001. *States of Imagination: Ethnographic Explorations of Post-Colonial State*. Durham, NC: Duke University Press.

Kothari, R. 1984. 'Non-Party Political Process'. *Economic & Political Weekly* 19 (5): 216–24.

Mahapatra, D. 2007. 'Right to Life Throttled in Nandigram'. *Times of India*, 19 November.

Melucci, A. 1988. 'Social Movements and the Democratisation of Everyday Life'. In *Civil Society and the State*, edited by J. Keane. London: Verso.

Melucci, A. 1989. *Nomads of the Present: Social Movements and Individual Needs in Contemporary Times*. Philadelphia, PA: Temple University Press.

———. 1995. 'The New Social Movements Revisited: Reflections on a Sociological Misunderstanding'. In *Social Movements and Social Classes: The Future of Collective Action*, edited by L. Malhue. London: SAGE.

Mohanty, R. 2003. 'Save the Chilika Movement: Civil Society Interrogating the State and the Market'. In *Does Civil Society Matter? Governance in Contemporary India*, edited by R. Tandon and R. Mohanty. New Delhi: SAGE.

———. 2007. 'Rights, Citizenship and State Accountability: Contentious Claims of Industry over Tribal Land'. In *Citizen Participation and Democratic Governance*, edited by R. Tandon and M. Kak. Delhi: Concept Publishers.

Mohanty, R., and Tandon, R., eds. 2006. *Participatory Citizenship: Identity, Exclusion, Inclusion*. New Delhi: SAGE.

Mohapatra, L. L. 1991. 'Development for Whom? Depriving the Dispossessed Tribals'. *Social Action* 41 (3): 271–87.

Mouffe, C. 2000. *The Democratic Paradox*. London: Verso.

Newell, P. 2006. 'Corporate Accountability and Citizen Action: Companies and Communities in India'. In *Participatory Citizenship: Identity, Exclusion, Inclusion*, edited by R. Mohanty and R. Tandon. New Delhi: SAGE.

Offe, C. 1985. 'New Social Movements: Challenging the Boundaries of Institutional Politics'. *Social Research* 52 (4): 817–68.

Omvedt, G. 1993. *Reinventing Revolution: New Social Movements and the Socialist Tradition in India*. New York, NY: M.E. Sharpe.

Oommen, T. K. 2004. *Nation, Civil Society and Social Movements: Essays in Political Sociology*. New Delhi: SAGE.

Pathak, A. 1994. *Contested Domains: The State, Peasants and Forests in Contemporary India*. New Delhi: SAGE.

Planning Commission. 1951. *First Five Year Plan*. Government of India, New Delhi.

Ranga Rao, A. B. S. V., and Kumar, S. 2003. *Multi-Party Accountability for Environmentally Sustainable Industrial Development: The Challenge of Active Citizenship. A Study of Stakeholders in the Simhadri Thermal Power Project, Paravada, Visakhapatnam District, Andhra Pradesh*. Department of Social Work, Andhra University, Visakhapatnam.

Sanhati. n.d. *November in Nandigram: A Citizen Report.* Available at http://sanhati.com

Shiva, V. 1989. *Staying Alive: Women, Ecology and Development.* London: Zed Books.

Tata Institute of Social Sciences (TISS). n.d. *The Sardar Sarovar Project: Experiences with Resettlement and Rehabilitation.* A Survey Report prepared by the Monitoring and Evaluation Team for Maharashtra, 1987–93, Bombay.

Touraine, A. 1985. 'An Introduction to the Study of New Social Movements'. *Social Research* 52 (4): 749–87.

3

National Rural Employment Guarantee Act

Access and Inclusion in Development

In the overall scenario of neoliberal growth and a free market economy, MGNREGA, popularly known as NREGA, has been designed to provide the poor and socially vulnerable populace the much desired social protection, welfare, work and assurance of livelihood, all rolled into one. Stated as the biggest anti-poverty programme in the world, NREGA has sought to extend the state patronage against the ruthlessness of the market. It has sought to restore local livelihoods and dependency on agriculture at a time when growth projects are displacing rural communities from their land and habitat. It has sought to compensate for the ill effects of the growth projects by being directly opposite in terms of providing the poor the much desired safety net.[1]

NREGA is different from earlier anti-poverty programmes by being rights-based and demand-based. At the outset, NREGA guarantees a minimum 100 days of wage employment in a year to a rural household that registers demand for work. NREGA, however, is not merely about work and employment; it puts the idea of sustainable rural livelihood at the core of poverty reduction. The creation of durable livelihood assets through land development, irrigation facilities, drought proofing and agro-forestry are critical components of NREGA. NREGA targets the Scheduled Castes (SCs), Scheduled Tribes (STs), women, landless persons and small and marginal farmers. NREGA was enacted in 2006 and has been in operation since. NREGA is implemented through decentralized governance of panchayat institutions. Panchayats are to plan the work, prepare labour budget and directly implement 50% of the work cost-wise.

NREGA has spent 3,116.54 billion since its inception out of which, 70% is spent on wages. A total of 0.13 billion households have job cards and close to 0.28 billion are engaged as workers. Of 57% public work undertaken under NREGA includes 43% on natural resource management, such as land development, water conservation and forestry, and 14% includes individual assets for the vulnerable population. More than 64% of total expenditure on agriculture and agriculture related work includes 42% on irrigation. Even though SC and ST participation as workers has remained low, women participation has increased from 40% in 2006–07 when the programme began to 57% by the end of 2015 (MoRD 2015, 2016).

How does a policy as ambitious as NREGA impact the rural poor? How do they experience it? How do they access the benefits? What does their inclusion mean to them? What outcomes

[1] NREGA, since its inception, has generated fierce debate between the neoliberals arguing against the state resources being put in safety net for the poor, labelling NREGA as dole to the poor, while the ardent champions of NREGA arguing for state provision for social protection, invoking the necessity and desirability of such a programme.

follow when a policy becomes distributive by including the poor and giving them access to benefits? The chapter discusses the distributive aspect of NREGA through the lens of access and inclusion. It does so by bringing in three facets of NREGA— social mobilization and how that connects people with NREGA; access to assets, particularly those related to agriculture and its impact on livelihood; and participation of women in NREGA and its impact on their lives.

NREGA has had a bag of mixed outcomes. There are cases of financial corruption and misappropriation (CAG 2012), unmet demands for work (Datta et al. 2012), delay in wage payment (MoRD 2012), absence of gram sabha where decisions are taken about work, weak monitoring system and absence of grievance redressal system (CAG 2012). There is a variation among states regarding NREGA performance, and some of the poorer states such as Uttar Pradesh, Bihar and Odisha have been lagging behind (MoRD 2014, 2015, 2016). Yet NREGA has led to wage employment that in turn has led to poor households' increased spending on food, health, loan repayment and children's education.[2] Assets created under NREGA, particularly irrigation and land development, have augmented agricultural productivity and livelihood opportunities (see the section on Agricultural Assets and Livelihood of Farmers in this chapter). NREGA's contribution in reducing the exploitation of labour, particularly agricultural labour, through minimum and fair wages as well as in checking migration in migration prone areas is evident (Banerjee 2010; Dreze and Khera 2011; MoRD 2012; UNDP 2015). There is high participation of women as wage labour in NREGA (see the section on NREGA and Inclusion of Women in this chapter).

The impact has not been universal across the country. However, in locations where they have occurred, the outcomes

---

[2] A large number of studies show the impact of NREGA employment on household spending (Banerjee and Saha 2010; Dasgupta and Sudershan 2011; Desai et al. 2015; Dreze and Khera 2011; Mishra et al. 2014; NCAER 2009).

indicate the potential of the policy to enhance livelihoods and bring people out from the poverty trap. Hence, despite all the aspects that point towards the difficult terrain people have to navigate to access their rights to work and livelihood promised through a policy document, the changes taking place at the grassroots also point out to the stirrings taking place in the villages in India by those who have remained unseen, invisible and voiceless and at the periphery and even outside of economic growth. NREGA has allowed people to contest the dominance and violence of development to claim what the state promises as social protection. Contrary to development being depoliticized, NREGA has deeply politicized people in the countryside.

Access to policy is highly contingent on local contexts. While a macro context can give people ambitious polices such as NREGA, whether a policy will be distributive in nature or will be appropriated by the powerful social groups depends on the local conditions. The micro-contexts, where people live, where their social and economic relations take place and where they interact with the state, influence policy outcomes. The policy outcomes are also contingent on the will and capacity of the local government. There is seldom a policy that has been accessed in a similar manner, or that has been distributive, across all locations. A host of local factors contribute to policy realization—local bureaucracy, panchayats, socio-economic relations, history of policy implementation and voice and demand from the vulnerable groups. The state–citizen interaction in particular locations holds the key to access and inclusion. Even when such local contexts are not documented, we can infer from the history of state–citizen interface that they are crucial (Mohanty 2014). A public policy is a complex instrument. While the macro trend can tell us the overall performance of the policy, how it works for the poor can be gleaned by taking into account micro contexts where it works, the groups for which it works and how the marginalized groups who are bypassed in the specific locations try to get entry.

A policy is a dynamic and complex interaction between the political opportunity structures (Gaventa and McGee 2009; Tarrow 1994, 1996) such as bureaucracy, institutions, laws, regulations and social opportunity structures (Mohanty et al. 2011; Thompson and Tapscott 2010) such as social relations, awareness, history of social mobilization and presence of CSOs. While the micro-political opportunity structures are instrumental in shaping polices, the microstructures may not respond to macrostructures.

As a policy, the documentation of NREGA is quite exhaustive. It has taken care of the minutest details from job application to monitoring of performance. To safeguard the policy from human errors, intended and unintended, technology has been used in such matters as job application through phone, 24-hour helpline and MIS to track performance. NREGA periodically updates its regulations to incorporate its own experiences. While it is a comprehensive policy, laid out in detail, yet it gets vitiated.

Hence, we find access to NREGA is low in certain states and localities such as in Uttar Pradesh as opposed to Andhra Pradesh. Andhra Pradesh has an effective decentralized network of *mandals* through which NREGA is implemented (NCAER 2009). Besides, the political commitment to NREGA is high in Andhra Pradesh (NCAER 2009). It is the first state to incorporate social audit proposed by the Mazdoor Kisan Shakti Sangathan (MKSS), the organization that pioneered social audit in Rajasthan. In Uttar Pradesh, and other states such as Odisha, Bihar and Jharkhand where NREGA has poor performance, there is administrative inefficiency and corruption and low commitment to NREGA (NCAER 2009). Social opportunity structures are crucial in locations where the political structures are weak or inefficient or inadequate. Rajasthan, one of the states where NREGA has been effective from the start of the project, has a vibrant presence of social mobilization, the MKSS being at the forefront of mobilizing workers in the Food for Work Programme long before NREGA was launched (Dreze and Khera 2011). However, if the state is not responsive then social mobilization can achieve little. How the state responds to a policy, whether it responds on its own or under pressure from citizens, determines how distributive the policy is. The procedural aspects of a policy, that is, how a policy is executed, have a bearing on the distributive aspects of a policy. For policies to be democratic in distribution, the procedures have to be democratic.

Civil Society and Social Mobilization

The history of social policies in India shows that access to policy requires organized effort by the social groups. Rajasthan, one of the states that generated work demands from the poor in the early phase of NREGA, points out the need for organized demand to access rights. NREGA gives people the right to work. However, a pronouncement of right per se does not mean that the rights will be granted. The rights remain inadequate unless demand is made on the state.

NREGA has intensified the potential of democratic politics from the side of marginalized social groups, particularly in contexts where (a) the hierarchies and inequalities are far too entrenched and where the local dominance resists the marginalized social groups' access to NREGA, (b) there is lack of political commitment from the government and (c) local bureaucracy poses obstacles. Civil society engagement and social mobilization have been one of the prominent features of NREGA wherein CSOs have been playing the crucial role of mediating between NREGA administration and the people.

For the marginalized groups, any effort to access state policy is an experience at several levels—understanding of their marginalization that deprives them from accessing policy, consciousness about rights and entitlement, interaction with the state officials, getting acquainted with the formal language of the state, occupying the public spaces in the village and outside, making their voices heard, shedding the fear of the state, taking responsibility to support members of their communities and demonstrating capacity for leadership (Mohanty 2014). The mobilization in civil society has led the poor, illiterate and socially marginalized to demand NREGA work.

Before I move to discuss how CSOs mobilize people,[3] a few examples from the tribal villages where, as a result of mobilization,[4] people have demanded work and regular payment.

The Bhil tribals in a village named Nad that comes under Ranapura Block, Jhabua District in Madhya Pradesh, approached the panchayat, block officials and finally the district collector to demand work under NREGA. When the panchayat refused work, they moved to the block office, and when the block office did not assure work, they went to the district collector, who then sanctioned work (Khan and Kellogg n.d.). The Tharu tribes together with other residents in Ratni hamlet that comes under Gaunaha panchayat, West Champaran District, organized a public hearing meeting to discuss and demand work. The meeting was attended by the panchayat and officials from the block. As a result, not only job cards were distributed to people in Ratni, those people from an adjacent village who had come to the meeting to demand payment for their work, received their payment (WFS n.d.). The Santhal Tribe in Khijri village, Tesia Block in Giridih District, could make the panchayat not only plan for work under NREGA but also provide people employment, regular payment and work place facilities such as shed and drinking water (Kellogg n.d.). In these three cases, the poor could rise above their multiple deprivations and overcome their fear of the panchayat and other officials. This has not been an easy journey for them, but not impossible as well, when supported and mobilized by CSOs.

[3] The discussion draws from the author's interaction and communication with CSOs working on NREGA.
[4] The Poorer Areas Civil Society (PACS) Programme supported by the Department for International Development, UK, formed partnership with Indian CSOs to mobilize people to claim NREGA benefits.

Collectivization

Social mobilization begins with collectivization, that is, by bringing people who have similar interests together. NREGA collectives have been formed as village- or panchayat-based CBOs (community-based organizations). The collectives are constituted in several ways: collectives of Dalits, collectives of women or collectives with crosscutting membership such as workers. In many places, self-help groups (SHGs; micro-credit groups of women) that are already constituted under various government schemes are mobilized to demand NREGA work. Collectives provide people the strength and solidarity of purpose, the power for negotiation and support in cases of backlashes which are common when the powers collide.

Information and Awareness

One of the issues that consistently surfaces as an implementation obstacle is that people lack information (Ravallion et al. 2013; Shankar et al. 2011). A question that can be asked: Why a policy with such elaborate details to ensure adequate implementation runs into difficulty at the first step—information about the provisions contained in the Act? There are many ways in which NREGA seeks to provide information—wall writings, NREGA mates,[5] panchayats meetings, CSOs and website, etc., but still the information gap persists. Information about work available, procedures for written application for work, guidelines for job cards, norms for livelihood asset creations remain inadequate. Lack of information can work to the disadvantage of the poor in two ways: It can deprive them of job and employment opportunities, and, at the same time, access to information by the powerful can lead to appropriation of benefits, thus making the poor doubly deprived (Shankar et al. 2011).

Information gap poses a crucial challenge to NREGA as it is a demand-driven programme, and demand generation depends

[5] NREGA has provision for recruiting mates locally whose responsibility is to communicate between the programme and the people.

on information about the provisions of the programme. Such information gap, particularly in the poor states of Bihar, Jharkhand, Odisha and Uttar Pradesh raises concern.

CSOs have been promoting information and awareness about NREGA by simplifying the guidelines. They have used popular methods such as posters, pamphlets, *nukkad natak* (street theatre), rallies and puppet shows to reach out to the non-literate and semi-literate people. Besides, regular meetings and door-to-door campaigns have also served as modes of communication about NREGA provisions. CSOs have collaborated with the government in organizing *rozgar divas* (employment day), *rozgar mela* (employment fair), NREGA camps and NREGA rallies. In Jharkhand, for example, the *Kaam Mango Abhiyan* (Demand for Work Campaign) is a joint initiative by the government and CSOs to mobilize people to demand work under NREGA. The inclusion of women as workers has been one of the strong features of NREGA. Supported by CSOs, women collectives, particularly SHGs, have been playing a key role in mobilizing women to register for work, plan projects in which more women can work, negotiate for recruitment of women as NREGA mate and demand for workplace facilities such as drinking water, shed and crèche.

Walking with the Workers

In putting in job applications for NREGA, there are instances where people still do not know that they are to get a written receipt of the application. Panchayats, if do not want to keep records of job application, do not provide receipts. To deal with the situation, technology is introduced; job request can be sent on mobile phones or can be registered on the helpline. Getting application registered is no longer a problem where these facilities are available, but it stops at that. It just gives people an assurance that they have been able to register for work, but there is no assurance of actual work. To avoid paying unemployment allowance, a few days of work are provided. As one person put it, 'Now it is no longer between two people where you can complain; now it is technology. So who do you complain against? Technology can make errors but you would not know exactly where the error has happened!' (personal communication).

CSOs provide hand holding support to NREGA workers at every step—registration for work and job card, ensuring the correct entry on the job card as well as on the muster roll, opening of accounts in post office, getting payments on time, applying for assets and supervision of assets created, registering complaints and follow ups.

Participation in Planning

NREGA intends to promote decentralized democracy by locating decision-making for planning and implementation with gram panchayats. NREGA requires panchayats to make an overall five-year plan and break it into year-wise units for the purpose of implementation. Given the rural profile of education/literacy and the unprecedented nature of technical skills NREGA requires for labour planning and budget, many panchayats, understandably, lack these abilities. Participatory planning at the grassroots is sabotaged in the absence of adequate knowledge about the technicalities of the scheme. Panchayat members have to seek the expertise of state officials: BDO, junior engineer (JE) and various line departments to make the plan. This not only breeds frustration among people who can never understand a policy in its totality but also increases the complicity of the powers that work against people's interests. CSOs support panchayats in preparing the perspective plan and labour budget even as they mobilize people to get their demands included in the planning process.

Interpretation of the State

Interpreting the complex texts of policy often deter people from engaging with the state in claiming rights. Yet for the state to respond, people have to articulate their demands in a language with which the state is familiar. Civil society performs the dual task of simplifying the state's language for people as well as enabling them to express themselves in a language that is comprehensible to state officials. Since NREGA is a complex policy, CSOs simplify the provisions in vernacular language for people. Through periodic trainings and interaction with village collectives, CSOs equip people with both the skill to interpret the official discourse on NREGA as well as to articulate in a language that can be comprehended by the officials. This involves a multitude of dimensions such as understanding the key norms of NREGA, filling up of demand forms, writing of applications, taking part in planning and operating post office and bank accounts. A particular challenge for CSOs is to build the skill of people who are semi-literate or non-literate. As many activities of NREGA demand literacy/language proficiency, CSOs assist people in engaging with a policy that, without their aid, would have remained beyond the access of the rural poor.

Interface with the State

The relationship between the state and its marginalized populace is characterized by patronage and protection as well as fear and intimidation. The state–citizen relationship is hierarchical as the state retains the power over its citizen. How do people walk into the domain of the state and interact with an entity that they have hitherto interacted with as a patron, but on whom they have demands to make as right-bearing citizens? What does this transformation entail? The transformation is difficult both from the side of citizens and from the side of the state, and it is this impasse that CSOs break when they interact both with the state and the citizen, and, importantly, bring both parties together to interact. CSOs organize interface meeting between people and government functionaries. This space, mutually constitutive of both the state and citizen, is vital for a policy such as NREGA. Neither do the government officials completely shed their power nor do people completely overcome their fear, yet through interfaces organized by CSOs, people push the barriers and gradually begin interacting with the government officials on their own.

Social Audit: Monitoring and Vigilance

Social audit is a tool in the hands of people to demand account-ability from the government. It is a tool to ensure democracy in social policies. Social audit is a community-led audit of NREGA that includes the audit of activities undertaken by NREGA, such as registration for work and job cards, issuance of job cards, work generated, number of assets created and expenditure incurred. Verification of muster roll and testimonials of people who work as wage workers or have benefited from the assets created under NREGA are critical for social audit. Social audits are conducted by gram sabha members. The findings are shared in a public meeting that is attended by community members, panchayat representatives, representatives from implementing agencies and eminent citizens. Social audit tests the effective-ness and inclusiveness of NREGA.

Social audit was pioneered by the MKSS. The first ever social audit of NREGA was conducted by the MKSS in Bhilwada District of Rajasthan in 2009. Andhra Pradesh was the first state to incorporate social audit in NREGA. Subsequently, NREGA has made social audit mandatory. CSOs are engaged by the NREGA administration to conduct social audit twice a year.

CSOs provide trainings on social audit, support community members to conduct audit and share the findings in public. Since social audits expose corruption and the power nexus in NREGA, they are a challenging process. CSOs play the critical role of providing support when people are threatened during the audit process.

CSOs have helped expand the developmental spaces and access to policy for the poor. Working both with the govern-ment and outside of it, CSOs have been mobilizing people to claim their rights. NREGA has sought collaboration with CSOs for social mobilization, particularly in awareness generation for work demand and social audit, yet this partnership is not without its share of tension with the government officials. It indicates that collaboration is not always supported at every level of the state apparatus. However, within the sphere of state mandated policies and institutions, CSOs stretch the boundaries to accommodate the interest of the poor.

Agricultural Assets and Livelihood of Farmers

NREGA has provision for livelihood assets creation on community as well as individual land belonging to small and marginal farmers, SC and ST, beneficiaries of land reforms and other rural poor.[6] Agricultural assets related to agriculture include micro and minor irrigation work, water conservation, renovation of traditional water bodies, land development and afforestation and plantation. A convergence approach is adopted where other government-sponsored programmes for livelihood and natural resource management such as watershed development are converging with NREGA.

Assets created under NREGA reflect suitability to local conditions. In Jharkhand, NREGA has prioritized wells. In Madhya Pradesh, NREGA has been converged with Kapildhara, a water resources scheme, and has created water structures for irrigation.

---

[6] Asset creation on private land is sanctioned for (a) SCs, (b) STs, (c) Nomadic Tribes, (d) Denotified Tribes, (e) other families below the poverty line, (f) women-headed households, (g) physically handicapped-headed households, (h) beneficiaries of land reforms, (i) the beneficiaries under the Indira Awaas Yojana and (j) beneficiaries under the STs and Other Traditional Forest Dwellers (Recognition of Forest Rights) Act, 2006 (2 of 2007), and after exhausting the eligible beneficiaries under the above categories, on lands of the small or marginal farmers as defined in the Agriculture Debt Waiver and Debt Relief Scheme, 2008, subject to the condition that such households shall have a job card with at least one member willing to work on the project undertaken on their land or homestead (MoRD 2015).

In Ladakh, Jammu and Kashmir, which is a dry area, NREGA has created a network of *kuhls* which are surface water channels in mountain areas. In Rajasthan, NREGA has constructed and revived traditional water harvesting structures called *johad*. In the dry and arid regions of West Bengal, mud-excavated structures called *happas* are constructed under NREGA.

Where productive assets are created, they have created livelihood choices and possibilities for the poor and excluded. Irrigation wells, check dams, village ponds and land development under NREGA have augmented the potential of agriculture. As a result, agricultural productivity and improved livelihood have accrued. Potential of assets created under NREGA, particularly irrigation and land development, in augmenting agricultural productivity and livelihood opportunities is observed and documented on specific locations.[7] Land and water related works have resulted in improvement in land quality, availability of water for irrigation, increase in irrigable land, increase in yield, diversification of cropping pattern, and a shift from subsistence farming to cash crops. By augmenting the potential of agriculture, NREGA has enhanced the livelihood of the poor farmers. It has also made farmers who had turned to wage labour return to agriculture. This shift has restored people's dignity.

Three examples: A farmer from Jharkhand who has benefited from a well on his land, a farmer from West Bengal who has benefited from a *happa* on his land, and two farmers from Maharashtra, one who has benefited from a farm pond on his

---

[7] Potential of assets created under NREGA, particularly irrigation and land development, in augmenting agricultural productivity and livelihood opportunities is observed and documented on specific locations: Odisha and Madhya Pradesh (CSE 2008); Madhya Pradesh (Mishra 2011); Andhra Pradesh (Kareemulla et al. 2009); Maharashtra (Narayanan et al. 2014); Andhra Pradesh, Karnataka, Madhya Pradesh, Rajasthan (IIS 2013); Jharkhand (Aggarwal et al. 2012; Bhaskar and Yadav 2011).

land and the other from a well, embankments and levelling of his land, are cited as illustrative of how farmers experience the benefits.[8]

Somra Oraon and Mura Khariya from Kumhariya Panchayat in Gumla District of Jharkhand have benefited from irrigation structures such as wells constructed under NREGA. Somra, like his fellow farmers in Dhangaon village, was dependent on monsoon and old wells in the village for irrigation. In Somra's own words,

> I had wanted to produce a combination of crops: Wheat, maize, peanuts, tomatoes, brinjal, cauliflower and other vegetables. But because of water unavailability, a large part of my land remained barren until the end of 2010. That was when I found out that MGNREGA could not just provide employment to me and my fellow villagers but also be a means to get a well dug on my land. (Das 2013)

A well dug on his land irrigates even the land that had been lying barren. In another village, Bangru, Mura describes the benefits of a well he constructed on his land under NREGA,

> Most farmers here grow paddy and all of us were dependent on the rains to irrigate our fields. But this year, even though the monsoon was delayed, none of us was late in our sowing. It was my new well that had made all the difference and it has plenty of water for everyone. (Das 2013)

Like Somra and Mura, Uttam Bauri, a farmer living in Bada Aral in West Bengal has befitted from the construction of *happa*. A *happa* measuring 36 × 40 feet has allowed him to cultivate vegetable such as tomatoes, brinjal, radish, cabbage and cauliflower in large quantities during the rabi season, as he is no

---

[8] The descriptions are taken from Das (2013), Sharma et al. (2010), and Narayanan et al. (2015).

longer dependent on the village pond for irrigating his land. Water from the *happa* also irrigates his land during kharif season when he grows rice.

> Uttam Bauri estimates that he has made a profit of Rs 5,000 to 6,000 from the sale of vegetables. Significant quantities of vegetables were also retained for household consumption. Uttam Bauri says that the water of the happa saved his kharif crop of rice. He would have otherwise lost his standard crop of 4 quintals to the drought. (Sharma et al. 2010, 15–16)

Experience of Ramesh Pawar and Sanjay Triambak from Triambak, Nashik, Maharashtra, who too were dependent on monsoon for agriculture and whose agricultural product increased due to irrigation facilities provided by farm pond, well and embankments constructed under NREGA, add to the stories of Somra, Mura and Uttam. While Ramesh constructed a farm pond under NREGA, Sanjay constructed a well and embankments; he also improved the quality of land through land levelling provided by NREGA. The irrigation support has enabled Ramesh to bring under cultivation the land that was lying barren.

> With the help of the pond, he has been able to cultivate paddy on all 9 acres of his land, revive a dying cashew and mango orchard, and plant a vegetable patch on which he grows brinjal and other leafy vegetables. He says the pond has reduced his dependency on the monsoon for sowing paddy and has also helped increase yields. He plans to try his hand at cultivating wheat next season as the pond allows him to draw water till January. (Narayanan et al. 2015, 23)

Sanjay uses the water from the well to cultivate rice, millet, onion and brinjal. 'He says that the well, along with other water conservation work, has allowed him to more than double his rice yields over the last 3 years. He also has a nursery set up under the Act next to his house' (Narayanan et al. 2015).

NREGA and Inclusion of Women

One of the key features of NREGA is women's participation as workers. Women's share in total person days generated under NREGA has increased from 40% during the first year 2006–07 to 57% in December 2015 (MoRD 2012, 2016). Person days for women increased from 0.364 billion in 2006–07 to 1.0357 billion in 2008–09, remained steady until 2010–11, and then increased to 1.1793 billion in 2011–12 and recorded at 0.6732 billion in December 2014. Although the quantum of total person days has declined, women's share has continued to increase (MoRD 2012, 2015).

NREGA has attracted both, women who have been working and earning wages and women for whom NREGA is their first employment. There are reasons why women are seeking employment in NREGA in large numbers. Women in rural areas mostly work as agricultural labour. Agricultural work is seasonal and there are lean period when work is not available. While men travel to nearby cities to work, women due to the responsibilities of taking care of the family prefer work closer to where they live and NREGA provides them work close to their villages.

What does it mean to women who work in NREGA? Does their employment translate into something more than an income? Can the financial inclusion of poor women in a government scheme transform their lives? Some of the critical implications for women's inclusion are as described in the following sections.

Minimization of the Chances of Labour Exploitation

As agricultural labour, women are paid lower wages than men for the same amount of work. Besides, in some places, wages are paid in kind, not in cash, and there is no regulation and discipline in payment. It is in this context with the limitations of working as agricultural labour that women enter NREGA (Grace and De Neve 2013; Nayak 2011). NREGA wages are paid through bank/post office account transfer and working hours are fixed.

Even when they work as labourers in NREGA, the work site gets a different connotation. It is not the private site of another person, who is more powerful, superior and, therefore, capable of exploitation, and who women have to obey in order to earn a livelihood. NREGA as a public work site is a government site (Nayak 2011). It is not owned by any person, but by the government. It is rule bound, gives equal wage to women and unlike village landlords and private contractors, NREGA does not challenge their dignity. NREGA is different in another significant way—the fear of sexual exploitation of women when working in private sites is absent. Hence, when looked through the lens of women, NREGA is not simply about the number of days of work and income but also the character and quality of the site where women work (Nayak 2011).

Entry of Women into Cash Economy

A dimension which has significant implication for women's identity, agency and gender equality is their entry into the formal labour force and cash economy. Women have not only remained underpaid in agricultural work, but their work, particularly when they work on homestead land or get paid in kind, is hardly recognized. NREGA recognizes and records their work as wage labour and thus makes possible the enumeration of women as part of the labour force. By paying women cash, NREGA enables their entry into the cash economy and cash-based transactions (Kelkar 2009). A recent survey indicates that 45% of women never received cash payment in their earlier work (Desai et al. 2015). By paying women cash and paying them at par with men NREGA brings equality into the labour market. Identification of women as formal labour and payment in cash gives women an identity not known even to many of them until they began working in NREGA. Cash payment brings women many benefits as they can readily meet their expenses; having cash also increases women's credit worthiness.

Financial Inclusion and Enhancement of Women's Well-being

NREGA has given women a feeling of 'well-being'. NREGA income enables women to spend on the basic needs of food, health, shelter, children's education and improve the standard of living of the family (Dasgupta and Sudershan 2011; Desai et al. 2015; Hirway n.d.; Jandu 2008; Pankaj and Tankha 2010; Mishra et al. 2014). Besides spending on basic needs, women's income enables them to send children to school and hire private tutors; important for them is also the ability to spend on health care as they can afford to pay for the doctor and medicine. Their income enables women to supplement family income where there are other earning members. Where a woman is the only earning member, her income assures the family of the bare minimum such as food, shelter and clothing. The prospects of work help them in planning expenditure, infuse them with optimism and save them from falling into distress and despondency. Women often handover their income to the head of the household or husband, yet they are able to retain certain amount with them. This enables them to influence decision-making within the household as also the autonomy to spend the portion of the income they retain. To quote Pankaj and Tankha (2010, 51),

> The large number of women who retained either part or whole of their NREGS wages, also retained choice over their use. They used it for all kinds of purposes: on daily

consumption items, household durables, health and education of children, visiting relatives, and on social ceremonies, etc. They also used it to meet their personal needs. The most common items of personal need women spent on included clothes, cosmetics and bangles, personal health (medicines), visiting relatives and giving gifts at the time of marriage and festivals to near and dear ones. The significance of this lies in reduced dependence on male and other family members.

Desai et al. (2015, 5) point out to another significant outcome for women workers,

> The growth in women's ability to freely seek health care rose from 66% to 80% in female participant households, whereas for all other households it rose by barely 10% points. In 2011–12, women from households in which women worked in MGNREGA were the most likely to feel free to visit a health centre alone.

Awareness About Self and Identity

Women, caught on the one hand in the hierarchies of gender and caste and, on the other, in the web of poverty, experience multiple levels of marginalization that impact upon their sense of self-esteem and identity. NREGA has the potential to reinforce a positive self-image in multiple ways: (a) having a job card and post-office account of their own gives women a sense of identity. The recognition from the formal systems of government and post-office brings certain kind of pride and confidence; (b) self-confidence and self-esteem comes through both, struggles for work and the results of struggle that have brought economic benefits and associated benefits that come with a rise in income; (c) equality in wage and equal opportunity for work is a big step towards equality;

(d) being able to interact with government officials and being able to negotiate for work brings women a new identity outside the spaces of home and family, the traditionally designated spaces for women; (e) being able to contribute towards family expenses; and (f) realizing their own needs such as new clothes, jewellery, soaps, hair oil, etc., and being able to purchase from their own income infuses them with a sense of self-awareness.

Consciousness About Rights and Entitlements

What does it mean for women who occupy a low position in the socio-economic hierarchy to get acquainted with the language of rights and actively pursue it? For most women, this brings a new consciousness about the legalities that govern their lives but about which they had very little or almost no idea. With NREGA, women are getting familiar with new vocabulary such as the Constitution, courts, governance and accountability, etc. CSOs have been mobilizing women to demand work, thus making them aware about the specific rights NREGA contains. This awareness does not remain confined to NREGA. Women in many places have gone beyond it to gather information about other entitlements such as housing, PDS, as also what specific rights they have as women, for example, their rights in situations of domestic violence or dowry. Whether they become successful or not, critical from the point of view of women are awareness and information about rights and entitlements that open up a new world for them and infuses them with the agency to pursue these. It is possible to discern the element of agency, which, if NREGA reaches out to women proactively, may enable them to see themselves not as beneficiaries of a patronizing state but as citizens who can make demands on the state and access what the state provides in the form of rights and entitlements.

Occupying the Public Space

Due to the nature of their occupation, women have been visible outside their homes, and, in that sense, they are not new to the public space. The public space, however, is infused with new meaning as new identities and new roles are created by NREGA. Until NREGA came to their villages, women have been visible only as wage labours. Getting connected with a policy such as NREGA has expanded the notions of the public space for women. Women are now visible in campaigns and rallies articulating their demands, and their spatial mobility has increased from village to block and from block to district. Women are visibly interacting with government officials, thus shedding their inhibition and fear of government.

Being able to talk directly to men, who are in positions of power, holds particular significance for women. It makes women transcend the boundaries of power in multiple ways: by breaking the cultural barriers of gender in a village setting where women seldom talk to men outside their homes; by transcending the barriers of caste where men holding official positions are from high castes with whom low caste and tribal women seldom interact; and by transcending the barriers of formal official boundaries where men hold positions and women are often considered as inferior and subordinate and have restricted access to such offices (Mohanty 2014). Women are visible in spaces such as banks and post offices where many of them are new members, and they are visible in social audits exercising their power to make governance accountable.

The aforementioned experiences are not without their share of frustration as women have to deal with the irregularities of NREGA such as job card, delay in payment, lack of work, and lack of workplace facilities. Yet women have joined NREGA in large numbers. As a public work and economic security policy, NREGA may not lead to obvert changes in the structural relations of power in the sphere of caste, economy or culture in which women are trapped and their consequent powerlessness emanating from their subservient position, but a policy like

NREGA can lead to many subtle changes in gender inequality and help women experience their position differently. Equality in wages, for example, paying women on par with men can have far reaching consequences in promoting gender equality.

A social policy such as NREGA may not lead to radical restructuring of social power. What it does is bring subtle changes by creating spaces for the poor and socially excluded to assert, negotiate and get their voice across. A policy per se is not a guarantee that it will be distributive even though it contains the possibilities for that. Political structures and social structures in varying degrees and through mutual interaction create conditions for access and inclusion. When development becomes distributive and includes the poor and give them access to benefits, the outcomes not only lift people from the poverty web in which their lives are entangled but also restore dignity and create a sense of empowerment, which is never complete, yet is not without substance.

References

Aggarwal, A., Gupta, A., and Kumar, A. 2012. 'Evaluation of NREGA Wells in Jharkhand'. *Economic & Political Weekly* 47 (35): 24–27.

Banerjee, K., and Saha, P. 2010. 'The NREGA, the Maoist and the Development Woes of the Indian State'. *Economic & Political Weekly* 45 (28): 42–47.

Bhaskar, A., and Yadav, P. 2015. *All is Well that ends in a Well: An Economic Evaluation of MGNREGA Wells in Jharkhand*. Report Submitted to National Institute for Rural Development Hyderabad by the Institute for Human Development, Eastern Centre, Ranchi, Jharkhand.

Comptroller and Auditor General of India (CAG). 2012. *Performance Audit of MGNREGA, 2007–2012*. New Delhi: CAG, Government of India.

Center for Science and Environment (CSE). 2008. *NREGA: Opportunities and Challenges*. New Delhi: CSE.

Das, P.P. 2013. 'NREGA can Touch People's Lives by Going beyond Just Giving them Jobs'. *The Weekend Leader*, 4 (3). Available at: http://www.theweekendleader.com/Culture/1486/bright-side.html

Dasgupta, S., and Sudershan, R. 2011. 'Issues in Labour Market Inequality and Women's Participation in India's Rural Employment Guarantee Programme'. Working Paper, Policy Integration Department, International Labour Office, Geneva.

Datta P., Murgai, R., Ravallion, M., and Walle, D. 2012. 'Does India's Employment Guarantee Scheme Guarantee Employment?' *Economic & Political Weekly* 47 (16): 55–64.

Desai, S., Vasistha, P., and Joshi, O. 2015. *Mahatma Gandhi National Rural Employment Guarantee Act: A Catalyst for Rural Transformation.* New Delhi: National Council for Applied Economic Research.

Dreze, J., and Khera, R. 2011. 'The Battle for Employment Guarantee'. In *The Battle for Employment Guarantee*, edited by R. Khera. New Delhi: Oxford University Press.

Gaventa, J., and McGee, R., eds. 2009. 'Making Change Happen: Citizen Action and National Policy Reform'. In *Citizen Action and National Policy Reform.* London: Zed Books.

Grace, C., and De Neve, G. 2013. 'Women at the Crossroads: Information of Employment Guarantee Scheme in Rural Tamil Nadu'. *Economic & Political Weekly* 48 (52): 83.

Hirway, I. n.d. *MGNREGA and Women Empowerment.* New York, NY: UN Women.

Indian Institute of Science (IIS). 2013. *Environmental Benefits & Vulnerability Reduction through MGNREG Scheme.* Bangalore: IIS.

Jandu, N. 2008. *Employment Guarantee and Women's Empowerment in Rural Area.* Available at http://www.righttofoodindia.org/data/navjyoti08_employment_guarantee_and_women%27s_empowerment.pdf

Kareemulla, K. Reddy, S. K., Rao, C. A., Kumar, S., and Venkateswarlu, B. 2009. 'Soil and Water Conservation Works through NREGS in Andhra Pradesh: An Analysis of Livelihood Impact'. *Agricultural Economics Research Review* 22: 443–50.

Kelkar, G. 2009. *Gender and Productive Assets: Implications of National Rural Employment Guarantee for Women's Agency and Productivity.* Paper presented at the FAO-IFAD-ILO Workshop on Gaps, Trends and Current Research in Gender Dimensions of Agriculture and Rural Employment: Differentiated Pathways out of Poverty.

Kellogg, S. n.d. *Santhal Tribals Put Khijri on the National Map.* Women's Feature Service. Available at http://wfsnews.org/freeread4.html

Khan, N., and Kellogg, S. n.d. *Learning to Demand MGNREGA Work: Bhil Tribals Show the Way.* Women's Feature Service. Available at http://wfsnews.org/freeread6.html

Ministry of Rural Development (MoRD). 2012. *MGNREGA Sameeksha: An Anthology of Research Studies, 2006–12.* New Delhi: MoRD, Government of India.

————. 2015. *Mahatma Gandhi National Rural Employment Guarantee Act, 2005: Report to the People.* New Delhi: MoRD, Government of India.

————. 2016. *Mahatma Gandhi National Rural Employment Guarantee Act, 2005: The Journey of a Decade.* New Delhi: MoRD, Government of India.

Mishra, R., Vishwanath, P. K., and Bhattarai, M. 2014. *Impact of MGNREGA Programme on Income, Assets creation, and Food Security: Evidence from Select 10 Semi Arid Tropic (SAT) Villages in India.* Paper Submitted for Presentation at a National Seminar on 'Flagship Programmes: Impact, Problems & Challenges Ahead', 19–21 November. National Institute of Rural Development, Hyderabad.

Mishra, S. K. 2011. 'Asset Creation in MGNREGA: A Study in Three Districts of Madhya Pradesh'. *Indore Management Journal* 3 (3): 19–30.

Mohanty, R. 2014. 'Mobilizing for Democracy: Civil Society Mediation and Access to Policy in India'. In *Mediating States and Citizens: Representing the Marginalized in the Global South*, edited by L. Piper and B. Von Liere. London: Palgrave Macmillan.

Mohanty, R., Thompson, L., and Coelho, V. S. 2011. 'Mobilizing the State? Social Mobilization and State Interaction in India, Brazil and South Africa'. Working Paper 359, Institute of Development Studies, Brighton.

Narayanan, S., Ranaware, K., Das, U., and Kulkarni, A. 2014. *MGNREGA Works and Their Impact: A Rapid Assessment in Maharashtra.* Mumbai: Indira Gandhi Institute of Development Research.

National Council of Applied Economic Research (NCAER). 2009. *Evaluating Performance of Mahatma Gandhi National Rural Employment Guarantee Act.* New Delhi: NCAER.

Nayak, N. 2011. 'Women Workers and Perception of the NREGA'. In *The Battle for Employment Guarantee*, edited by R. Khera. New Delhi: Oxford University Press.

Pankaj, A., and Tankha, R. 2010. 'Empowerment Effects of the NREGS on Women Workers: A Study in Four States'. *Economic & Political Weekly* 45 (30): 45–55.

Ravallion, M., van de Walle, D., Dutta, P. Murugai, R. 2013. 'Testing Information Constrains on India's Biggest Anti-poverty Programme'. World Bank Policy Research Working Paper 6598.

Shankar, S., Gaiha, R., and Jha, R. 2011. 'Information, Access and Targeting: The National Rural Employment Guarantee Scheme in India'. *Oxford Development Studies* 39 (1): 69–95.

Sharma, V., Mit, R., and Ghosh, S. 2010. 'An Effort to Make Water Everybody's Business'. *News Reach* 10 (5).

Tarrow, S. 1994. *Power in Movement: Social Movements, Collective Action and Politics*. New York, NY: Cambridge University Press.

———. 1996. 'States and Opportunities: The Political Structuring of Social Movements'. In *Comparative Perspective on Social Movements: Political Opportunities, Mobilizing Structures and Cultural Framings*, edited by D. McAdams, J. D. McCarthy, and M. N. Zald. Cambridge: Cambridge University Press.

Thompson, L., and Tapscott, C. 2010. 'Introduction: Mobilization and Social Movements in the South- the Challenges of Inclusive Governance'. In *Citizenship and Social Movements: Perspectives from the Global South*, edited by L. Thomson and C. Tapscott. London: Zed Books.

United Nation Development Programme (UNDP). 2015. *MGNREGA Sameeksha II: An Anthology of Research Studies*, 2012–2014. New Delhi: UNDP.

Women's Feature Service (WFS). n.d. *Eight Years after MGNREGA: Ratni Village Wakes to its Benefits*. Available at http://wfsnews. org/freeread5.html

4

Participatory Governance

The Paradoxes of Development and Democracy

Over the past two decades, states around the world have been promoting participatory local democracy through new institutional forms of local governance. These institutions have opened up possibilities for grassroots participation in shaping development and governance. In India, the participatory governance institutions called panchayats were reinvigorated in rural areas in the year 1992.[1] Panchayats are responsible for ensuring economic development and social justice for the poor and socially marginalized rural population. The representation of low castes, tribal and women in panchayat is sought through affirmative action, that is, their membership is guaranteed by

[1] The panchayat system existed earlier; it was energized as a system of decentralized governance and as an institutional arrangement for participatory governance.

reserving a third of seats for Dalits, a third for tribals and a third for women.

For development to be democratic, the institutions have to be democratic. How democratic are the institutions for the poor and the socially marginalized? Are the institutions, through the execution of development, capable of addressing the goal of social justice? These two overarching questions lead to more questions: How does Dalit participation take place in the context of an entrenched caste society? To what extent development programmes within the panchayat promote social justice for Dalits? How do Dalits pursue social justice even as they work towards the execution of development programmes? How do development and social justice interact with each other in such contexts? Does greater access to development resources and benefits address the deep rooted issues of social justice?

The chapter engages with these questions to discuss the development–democracy dynamics as they take place within the panchayat institutions. The chapter draws from a study the author conducted during 2006–07 in the Sabarkantha District of Gujarat, where the deep-rooted practice of untouchability has left Dalits at the margins of society and polity.[2] In analysing the development and democracy interaction within the panchayat, the chapter discusses three critical dimensions: democracy within local governance institutions, democracy in social relations and democracy in the distribution of developmental resources to Dalits.

The chapter reveals how Dalit mobilization in panchayat institutions, spearheaded by local CSOs, enabled them to claim developmental benefits as well as social justice. While substantial gains occurred in the redistribution of developmental goods and services to Dalit communities, the institutions remained largely closed and resistant to accommodate Dalits as equal, and

[2] The study was conducted in the villages of Deoli, Jethipura, Netramali and Virpur in Idar Block of Sabarkantha District. The villages are heavily populated by Dalits.

the occasional Dalit assertion to equalize the social relations were yet to make their impact on the institutions. Social justice thus remained confined to access to developmental provisions of housing, road, water and electrification, etc. This raises many paradoxes of development and democracy as they unfold in the local governance institutions and the social setting where the institutions are located.

Participatory Governance and Dalit Participation

Participatory governance in the form of democratic decentralization has generated varieties of perspectives. Intuitionalist perspective (Crook and Manor 2000) privileges institutional structures and designs and argues that decentralized institutions will result in efficiency by erasing bottlenecks and delays. They will result in transparency by being open and easily accessible, accountable by virtue of being constituted by members from local communities and guarantee sustainability of projects by providing ownership to local people. Although there is a possibility of elites capturing the institutions and benefits going to those who are politically connected, over a period of time, decentralization will build people's capacities to engage, question and demand from the local governments. Institutional perspective draws heavily from World Bank's good governance agenda that privileges administrative efficiency in democracy promotion.

The intuitionalist perspective is critiqued by those who see decentralization as a political project. A process-oriented perspective (Cornwall and Coelho 2007) is less optimistic of the institutions per se and argues that processes taking place within the institutions are critical to determine whether and to what extent such institutions can promote democracy at the local level. Drawing from case studies conducted in South Africa, Bangladesh, India, Brazil in the South and United Kingdom and Canada in the North, Cornwall and Coelho (2007) provide a nuanced picture of what they call 'invited spaces'—the state institutions into which people are invited to participate. They raise such critical process-oriented issues as representation, participation, engagement with the state, dynamics in civil society and citizen action that influence local governance. Their argument that institutional structures and designs per se do not guarantee participation and democracy brings into focus local power dynamics and how these influence democracy agenda of local governance.

Heller (2001) too finds the institutional perspective too technocratic to ensure effective decentralized governance. Instead, he views decentralization as a political project that must result in redistribution of power horizontally by 'expanding the domain of collective action' and vertically by 'incorporating citizens'; it must result in shifts in power between state and society on the one hand and between those who have 'privileged access to the state and those 'newly empowered subordinate groups', on the other. Based on his study in Porto Alegre, Kerala and South Africa, Heller argues that democratic decentralization requires both a strong state with the political will to push for decentralization and a strong civil society to mobilize and build citizen capabilities. A third requirement for successful decentralization, he argues, is the presence of a political party with a strong social movement base that can champion decentralization. Gaventa (2011) too views local governance fostering new and improved state–citizen relations. Local governance is a way of doing both: making the state responsive and enhancing citizen participation. Together they create possibilities for deepening of democracy, actualization of rights and citizenship and equitable distribution of development.

Although there is no disagreement on desirability of decentralization, studies have pointed many gaps between expectations and actual outcomes. Robinson (2003) finds from his multi-country study that service delivery outcomes of decentralization have been below the mark both in terms of quality and in terms of equity. Another multi-country study (Crook and Sverrisson 2001) also reports the absence of pro-poor outcomes from decentralization except in the Indian state of West Bengal and some part of Brazil, and, in both the cases, the success was more to do with strong national and state governments than local. The champions of decentralization are cautioned of elite capture of local governance (Bardhan and Mukherjee 1999) and also that couching local governance in terms of trust, reciprocity, network and association can divert attention away from powerful vested interests hijacking local governance, and promote an apolitical view of decentralization (Harriss 2002).

Panchayats in rural areas were consolidated as units of local governance through the 73rd Constitutional Amendment in 1992. Understood variously as the grassroots units of governance, village republic and local governance, panchayats are part of a three-tier system of governance that begins at the village and ends at the district. Each panchayat consists of several revenue villages and hamlets, and is divided into several wards from which candidates are elected to a panchayat. These members are referred to as ward members/panch and the head of the panchayat is called sarpanch/gram pradhan. Gram sabha or the village council, which is the general body of all the adult residents in the villages which constitute a panchayat, is the body to which the panchayat members are accountable. A third of the seats in each panchayat are reserved for low castes, tribal and women. That, however, does not obstruct them from contesting election from open seats.

Participatory governance at the village level reflects the broader vision of national development. Democratic decentralization is thus guided by the twin objectives of economic development and social justice. The institutions are set up to revamp the equitable and efficient provisioning of development goods and services such as water, electricity and roads as well as wages and livelihood resources. All development and social security programmes of the central government as well as provincial governments are implemented through panchayats. With a decentralized budget and decision-making, it is envisioned that effective delivery of goods, services and resources will take place. Along with delivering development, the institutions are also conceived to promote social justice among the rural populace, that is, social equality is a mandate for the local governance institutions even as they execute economic development. Affirmative action and reservation of membership for women, lower caste and tribals within panchayat institutions are conceived as mechanisms to disperse social power through local government. Additionally, there are social justice committees (SJC) within panchayats to focus on the issues of social justice.

Apart from giving Dalits entry into the panchayat through affirmative action and formal legitimization of their 'power' within the panchayat, the state does not do much to ensure that Dalits exercise that power to their advantage. Despite being conceived and formalized as participatory and inclusive institutions, there is, in fact, nothing inherent in the local governance institutions to prevent them from continuing to reinforce the social stereotypes of caste and gender. In fact, the exercise of power by the powerless groups in the same social setting that tries to keep them forever subservient intensifies and provokes caste violence as a response. Quite frequently, the violence manifests within the institutional spaces of local governance.

Situated in the very context from where the members are drawn, local institutions can hardly transcend the structural positioning that conditions social relations around the issues of caste. Who is treated with respect? Whose voice is heard? Who carries authority? Who takes decisions? These matters are decided not so much by the power a member holds within the panchayat as by the already existing relations of social power that determines the subjectivity of the members. It is a reflection of existing social relations when Dalit members, particularly Dalit women, are subjected to verbal abuse in panchayat meetings. Such instances are often ignored by the panchayat secretary, who is a lower-level administrator from the block administration and whose responsibility is to attend the meetings and write up the minutes.

The development schemes for Dalits do not invite much resistance from the upper castes as there is no possibilities of appropriating the resources. Besides, in the early years of panchayat, Dalits were seldom aware of such provisions. However, when there were schemes such as housing, employment, water, health and electricity supply that are not superficially marked for any social group but could be accessed by all the poor in the village, there was resistance to Dalits demanding the goods and services. Even when the upper castes are economically better off, they still resist the benefits going to lower castes. Sharing of power within the panchayat is resisted as it means giving them equal status and strengthening the Dalit voice within panchayat.

The following two quotes from Sabarkantha illustrates how the upper castes still retain power within the panchayat. Talking about the Bhavnagar Panchayat in Idar Block in Sabarkantha District, Tapas Satpathy (2006, 54) writes,

The dominant castes invited a Dalit to be the sarpanch (chairperson) only on the condition that he would not sit on the same chair meant for the sarpanch and would not drink tea from the same cups used to serve the members of the dominant castes. Simultaneously a person from the dominant caste became the upsarpanch (deputy chairperson). Hence, the actual powers remained with the dominant castes and the role of the Dalit sarpanch was limited to signing bills and other papers of the panchayat under the direction of the upsarpanch.

As Manjula, the Dalit sarpanch of Deoli village in Idar Block, who has to face a lot of verbal abuse in the panchayat, puts it,

Of course, the high caste people have no choice but to vote a Dalit into power when the rules are set for that. But then they want someone who they can dictate and keep subservient. Since I am not much educated and I was never visible in the public life of the village, they assumed that I would obey them in every respect. Being a Dalit and being a woman I was socially vulnerable. But when I got into the position of a sarpanch I realized that I could do so much for my people. And the high caste people never liked it. (personal communication)

In another context, writing about how the upper castes reacted to their loss or the Dalits' gain from panchayat system and how the upper castes misconstrue the local governance arrangements, Sumathi and Sudarsen (2005, 3754) quote a well-off upper caste man from a village of Tamil Nadu: 'Donate the country to the communists so that everyone drink kanji (rice gruel) and equality could be maintained'. The man reacting adversely to Dalit entry into panchayat 'equates the principles of a positive discrimination of political participation at the grassroots level to communism'.

The upper caste reaction to Dalit participation in panchayat has manifested as resistance, sabotage, physical violence and sometimes to strike a balance of power within the panchayat to render the Dalits as proxy members. However, the resistance has not gone unchallenged. As Morris et al. (2008, 129) observe in Rajasthan:

> These dalit women are chosen not on the basis of their individual performance or potential to emerge as effective village leaders, but because men believe that dalit women will be easy to manoeuvre and can be used to wield power. However, in the specific instances when these women have chosen to exercise their power, assert their authority, men have swiftly moved in with no-confidence motion to remove them.

They also observe:

> There are more women leaders today who have begun to address public gatherings, chair panchayat meetings, negotiate with officials, monitor rolls, manage accounts, facilitate community based monitoring of and access to basic services and mobilize women and the community to participate in public forums to enhance accountability. (2008, 118)

The women in this context challenged the upper caste conspiracy, albeit in another location within the same state, and continued to hold office.

When the political will of the state ceases with the declaration of formal guidelines and institutional framework for panchayats, it is not unlikely that the agenda of Dalit political participation in the local institutions will suffer for the reasons mentioned earlier. As could be expected, this happened in the Sabarkantha villages. Dalit aspirations to take advantage of this constitutional provision resulted in serious backlashes when the upper castes retaliated, especially when the Dalits questioned inequality and exclusion. Without little intervention by higher government institutions and authorities to support Dalit efforts, the panchayats remained the bastion of upper castes. As a result, the SJCs that were constituted as part of the panchayat system to address the issues of social justice remained only on paper.

Participatory Governance and Dalit Mobilization in Sabarkantha

Social justice is a ubiquitous concept in the state's definition of liberal democracy in India (Mahajan 1998). In the pan-Indian framing of social justice, fuelled by a liberal democratic ethos, it finds expression in two different forms—fundamental rights and directive principles of state policy. Fundamental rights are inalienable rights guaranteed by the Indian Constitution; directive principles are directives and guidelines that inform state policies for development. If a person's fundamental rights are violated, they can seek judicial protection of these rights; the directive principles are not enforceable through court intervention. For instance, the laws against untouchability and the right to equality in public spaces fall within the domain of fundamental rights, whereas affirmative action, equal and fair wage, and fair allocation of developmental goods and services are the domain of directive principles.

Dalit mobilization in India has a long and chequered history (Ilaiah 2001; Omvedt 1994, 2001, 2003; Pai 2002; Shah 1994, 2001; Zelliot 2001). Their mobilization has sought to address a variety of issues such as caste inequalities and atrocities by upper castes, low economic status and poverty among Dalits,

their cultural marginalization within Hindu culture, their entitlement to fair wages and decent living conditions, and their
right to live with dignity. In addressing these issues, Dalits have
taken to diverse methods such as forceful temple entry to break
the caste norms that do not allow them to enter Hindu religious
places, mass conversion to Buddhism to escape the exploitative
Hindu caste and religious system, cultural mobilization to establish the distinct identity of Dalit culture and the organization
of Dalit political parties to capture the state power.[3] Through
these methods, Dalits have mounted a vociferous criticism of
caste and have taken action against the caste hierarchy and the
resultant inequalities that follow and permeate every aspect of
their living and that shape their relations with the powerful
including the state.

Dalit mobilization within the institutions of panchayat,
however, is recent and different from mobilizations mentioned
earlier. While it addresses the old and hitherto unresolved issues
of social exclusion and social justice, the mobilization takes
place not only within the institutions created by the state but
also Dalit entry into which is facilitated by the state directives
of affirmative action.

This entry into the state institutions of participatory governance, however, does not guarantee much unless Dalits make
claims about their rights, bring in their agenda and make their
own claims to rights and power, and make their presence visible. Since this mobilization takes place in and through the
state-created institutions, the institutional objectives and norms
influence the mobilization. Yet, it is not completely governed
by what the state offers; alternative ideas, imaginations and
politics shaped by the mobilization are also brought into
the state-created institutions to influence and expand them.
Nonetheless, the state framework of local governance prevails

[3] The Dalit movements, particularly in northern and southern India,
transformed themselves into political parties and entered mainstream
politics, thus making the low-caste movements as part of electoral politics in a democracy. This happened at the provincial and national level.

with its framing of development and social justice. This, as we will see in the subsequent sections, has given rise to paradoxes of development of democracy.

The recommendation to constitute SJCs as part of panchayat in Gujarat came first in 1972 by a special committee, known as Zinabhai Darzi Committee, formed by the then Government of Gujarat. The committee conceptualized SJCs to promote what it called 'democratic socialism', through democratic decentralization (GoG 1972). The members of SJCs were to be recruited from the elected members of panchayat, and, where such membership in the panchayat was found lacking, they were to be recruited from gram sabha. Two tasks were designed for the SJCs—taking part/pushing the agenda of fair the distribution of economic goods and opportunities and taking measures against social discrimination and atrocities committed against Dalits, tribals, women and other marginalized groups. These provisions were incorporated when Gujarat formulated its local governance legislation following the 1992 Constitutional Amendments. However, it could not make SJCs absolute in autonomy as was recommended by the Zinabhai Darji Committee. It made SJCs a subcommittee of panchayat giving it the authority to take decisions, but the panchayat has to ratify those decisions and allocate a budget for their implementation.

Sabarkantha is one of the 25 districts that comprise the state of Gujarat situated in the western part of India. The prominent caste groups that constitute the SC population in Sabarkantha are *vankar*, the weavers; *chamar*, those who clean dead animals; *chenba*, those who make baskets/mats from bamboo; *tirgar*, those used to make bows and arrows in the past; *turi*, the barbers, and they also beat drums during festivals; *garupandya*, those who perform religious rituals for Dalits; and *valmiki*, those who clean the garbage from the village. Valmikis are the lowest in the sub-caste hierarchy of the Dalits and are considered the lowest of the low. Dalits in addition to their caste occupation also work as wage labours. Some of them have small landholdings but the agriculture income is not sufficient. A large number of Dalits work as agricultural labour, construction workers and other forms of labour available in the region.

In Sabarkantha, the SJCs are formed by the state as part of local governance institutions to promote the agenda of social justice, which essentially means promoting the values of equality and participation as well as the egalitarian distribution of developmental resources so that the marginalized sections, importantly the Dalits can overcome dominance and exclusion. In principle, the panchayats are to work on the agenda of social justice by recruiting members from Dalit communities through election. One-third of the seats in each panchayat is reserved for Dalit members. Dalit members are to constitute the SJC with the approval of the head of panchayat, and the committee is responsible for extending the panchayat functions of economic development and social justice to Dalit communities.

The effort on the part of the Dalits to take advantage of this constitutional provision resulted in serious backlashes when the upper castes retaliated, often violently, to Dalits who questioned inequalities and exclusion. Without much intervention by the higher government institutions and authorities to support Dalit efforts, the panchayats remained the bastion of high castes until CSOs began addressing the issue. When panchayat elections were held in Gujarat in 2002, Unnati,[4] a CSO based in Ahmedabad, the capital city of Gujarat, took the initiative to mobilize the SJC members and Dalit communities for social justice. It worked with local organizations in the region to form a network of CSOs aptly named as Samajik Nyay Manch (SNM) as well as a network of SJC members to push the agenda of social justice within the panchayat institutions.

Unnati's interface with the panchayat began when it initiated the voter awareness campaign in Sabarkantha for raising awareness about panchayat elections scheduled for 2001. To facilitate the campaign, it formed a Panchayat Resource Centre in Khedbrahma Block of Sabarkantha District. During

[4] Unnati literally means progress.

the course of the campaign, Unnati interacted with both the elected members of panchayat and the communities. It worked in partnership with other CSOs in four blocks in Sabarkantha, namely, Idar, Prantij, Himatnagar and Modasa; subsequently, they came together to form the SNM, the civil society network which spearheaded the mobilization for social justice. The voter campaign made Unnati and its partners realize that social justice is a critical issue that needed focused intervention. Hence, the SNM was formed in 2002 with eight organizations to activate and energize SJCs by mobilizing Dalits. This inspired other CSOs in the district to join the network and four organizations from three other blocks—Vijay Nagar, Bhiloda and Vadali, joined the SNM. The network evolved into a vibrant one, which energized the Dalit agenda of social justice. It organized SJC chairpersons in clusters at block, district and finally in the province to galvanize support for Dalit mobilization. Through a mobilization strategy that organized Dalits to claim membership in the panchayat, bring in the issues of social injustice to the SJCs and the panchayat and to improve the practices at the local panchayat as well as the higher government institutions, the network helped in bringing the issues of social justice to the public space.

Dalit mobilization for social justice in local governance institutions in Sabarkantha as demonstrated by SNM was constitutive of three critical facets—strengthening the SJCs; mobilizing for redistribution of developmental provisions; and mobilizing for social equality and dignity.

Strengthening the SJCs

This dimension of the mobilization rests on the premise that Dalit participation and leadership in panchayat will be ensured if the institutions function efficiently. Institutional efficacy is often judged in terms of the efforts made to put in place the officially prescribed structures and processes.

After the panchayat elections were held in 2002, Unnati conducted a study on the status of SJCs in the district. The study found that SJCs were not formed in most villages and that, where they were, members were selected unanimously by the sarpanch and the panchayat secretary without any consultation with other panchayat members. SJC members selected through such a procedure had no information about the roles they were expected to perform in the panchayat system. Therefore, the first task for the SNM was to organize a meeting with the chairpersons of all the SJCs located in the eight blocks where the network CSOs worked. The first ever meeting of these SJCs, held together with the representatives of SJCs from the district, discussed the status of the village SJCs and strategies to activate them. Following the meeting, the SNM wrote to the BDO and the panchayat secretary to take steps to constitute SJCs. This initiative, supported and monitored closely by the SNM, led to the formation of SJCs in all the panchayats in the eight blocks of Sabarkantha District.

SJC members were mobilized through various capacity-building efforts that sought to equip them with information about their roles, rights and responsibilities within the panchayat system; they were also given training on social and governance-related issues in the region. To ensure that the SJCs function effectively, networks of SJCs were formed at the block, district, and later on, at the state level. Representatives from village SJCs were selected to form the block network, whose responsibility was to address the issues of social justice at the block through interface with the government officials. Representatives from the block network were selected to form the district network, with a mandate to address the issues coming from the villages and blocks. Subsequently, a state network of SJCs was formed by taking representatives from the district network. Social awareness campaigns were organized periodically, with rallies and cultural shows that included folk music and theatre. At the very beginning of the mobilization, in September 2002, a meeting was arranged between SJC members and the government representatives. A *sammelan* (large conference) was organized at the Himmat Nagar Town Hall, where approximately 1,500 people, including members of SJCs and

Dalit communities from different parts of Sabarkantha, come together to tell their stories to a group of ministers, in the presence of academics, the media and the CSOs.

Mobilizing for Redistribution of Developmental Provisions

Economic development as one of the prime objective of panchayat features in the agenda of SJCs, which have the responsibility to take care of the developmental needs of Dalit communities. SJCs in Sabarkantha actively pursued the developmental activities for their communities in getting critical services such as water and electricity connection to the Dalit households; land or house constructed under Indira Awas Yojana; construction of cement roads that connect Dalit habitats with the rest of the village and with the main road to the city; and getting Dalits to register in the BPL list so that they can take advantage of the government subsidies meant for the poorest of the poor. These developmental services are of critical importance to the well-being of Dalits. The SJCs' efforts to foster development were highly appreciated by their communities.

The developmental resources that SJCs brought to Dalits were from the redistribution of benefits from already existing government programmes rather than undertaking new initiatives. However, redistribution was viewed as an important achievement as the resourceful people in the village and in the panchayat had invariably appropriated the benefits keeping the Dalits outside of developmental services, and, on many occasions, the government authorities either supported this practice or remained indifferent to the needs of the Dalits. In addition, special programmes and funds earmarked for Dalits remained unutilized as Dalits were either unaware of them or could not pursue them on their own. In this context, the SJCs struggled hard within the panchayat to get the provisions for Dalit communities. In fact, the efficiency and success of the SJCs in distributing these developmental resources came to be seen as an indication of the strength of Dalit leadership within the panchayat and as a manifestation of Dalit needs, voices and decision-making within it.

Mobilizing for Social Equality and Dignity

What began as a mobilization to activate the political powers of the SJCs and to appropriate developmental schemes, goods and services for the low castes gradually begun to address issues of social discrimination, violence and abuse. The emphasis was on the material needs for Dalit economic empowerment, but along with that the SJCs pursued, what can be called 'claiming of social space'. They claimed burial space for Dalits in the village common land as well as cultural spaces for celebration of festivals. Social space was also claimed through behavioural and attitudinal changes consciously made by the Dalits themselves, for example, they chose not to sit on the floor when the upper caste members appropriated the chairs during panchayat meeting or not to eat off the plates kept separately for Dalits during village feasts. Another space-claiming activity was to have Dalits celebrate the festivals such as Holi (festival of colours) or Diwali (festival of lights) in the same place where the upper castes celebrated them. In a few cases, showing complete disregard for caste rules, the Dalits entered into the temples of upper castes.

All these radical acts added the dimension of 'dignity' to social justice. The right to live in a dignified manner and the right to be treated with dignity are emerging as strong claims by Dalit mobilization in contemporary times. Of all the ways of claiming equality and inclusion, dignity is the most radical claim as it strikes at the roots of a social system that discriminates a set of human beings as 'untouchables'. Dalit mobilization within local governance institutions, in Sabarkantha villages, demanded such symbolic assets as a separate office room for the SJC and a letterhead and a stamp bearing the name of the SJC. These symbolic assets helped Dalits establish their identity and gave them a feeling of power. The SJC members cited this as one of the achievements of their mobilization. Another way in which the Dalit members of panchayat claimed their identity and dignity was to spell out their caste surnames, which revealed their untouchable identity on the nameplates and letterheads, instead of hiding them.

Dalit mobilization in panchayat tells us that political, material and social aspects of their mobilization are intertwined and interact with each other in complex ways. Dalit groups living in the Sabarkantha villages have learnt that their struggle is manifold—tracking development schemes and funds for Dalits, channelling the benefits to Dalit habitats in the village and demanding identity and equality on a political and symbolic level, while at the same time striving to equalize the social spaces where the upper castes that control them have always discriminated against them.

Participatory Governance: Development and Social Justice

It is evident that granting of political power to Dalits and any consequent participation of Dalits in panchayat is rendered ineffective unless they themselves mobilize and assert their power. Dalit mobilization, represented through such activities as claiming political space within the panchayat, accessing state-sponsored developmental provisions to Dalit communities, forcing entry into the social space barricaded by the upper caste or capturing and animating the public space through the widening of networks and organization of huge demonstrations invoked Dalit identity and gave SJCs visibility in the public sphere. In villages where a panchayat was also headed by a Dalit, considerable cooperation was extended to SJCs even though Dalit members had to encounter hostility from upper caste members in both the panchayat and the village.

Dalit mobilization within the framework of participatory governance is indeed an intersection between two sets of imaginations—one that comes from the state-given meanings and the other formed by Dalits' current subjective experience as well as how they envision themselves in future. Dalits therefore strive for political power and the redistribution of developmental provisions of water, food, road and electricity, even as they continue to reconstruct social justice in terms of 'dignity' that signifies their need for equality, inclusion and respect. Framing social justice in terms of 'dignity' puts their mobilization in the context of atrocities and prejudices that Dalits are subjected to in the Hindu caste structure that treats them as 'untouchables'. Striving for dignity is a radical political imagination that does not find any place in the vocabularies of the state or formal democracy, but which Dalit mobilization has articulated in their quest for social justice.

This claiming of both political and social spaces, however, could not democratize the local institutions of participatory governance to be sufficiently inclusive of Dalits and their agenda of social justice. The charisma of individual activists and leadership pushed the Dalit agenda forward to a significant extent, but the institutions remained mostly closed.[5] Hence, even after considerable mobilization by Dalit members to give SJCs visibility, in the panchayat elections held in December 2006, SJCs had still not been formed in many panchayats or had been formed by the panchayat secretary in consultation with few panchayat members, thus repeating the history of 2002. Consequently, many Dalits were not even aware that they were nominated as SJC members in their own panchayats.[6]

The active members of SJCs, in most cases, were completely caught in organizing development resources for Dalits, most critically housing, water, electricity and roads. While the efforts made to redistribute basic material goods and services more evenly enables Dalits to live in dignity, the pursuits of

[5] The success of individual leadership was visible in almost all the SJCs we visited during our fieldwork. In fact, the individuals were so popular that, in the villages, people could tell us the name of the chairperson of SJC, but they could hardly tell who the other members were.

[6] Personal communication with Tapas Satapathy and members of SNM.

development limited the scope of social justice. Their address-ing of issues of social discrimination and atrocities thus raised suspicion among the higher echelons of power.

When asked to describe what constituted social justice, the members of SJCs listed a number of issues for Dalits: denial of burial ground to the Dalits; restrictions on their temple entry; cases of violence against their women; Dalits still carrying the traditional occupation of removing the dead animals from the village; low wages paid to them; and lack of decent housing, water provisions, electricity and good roads. The same mem-bers, when asked about the role of SJCs, enumerated all the developmental activities they had pursued or wanted to pursue. When probed a little deeper, they said that they also valued the distinct identity of SJCs because that gave Dalit communi-ties a stake in panchayat. They also recalled the efforts, few in number but critical nonetheless, that they made in address-ing the issues of social discrimination in their villages. Local government restricts democratic politics of Dalits, in that the official discourse limits the Dalit imagination to development issues. While a number of schemes and funds are created for Dalits, cases of social discrimination and atrocities are shrugged off as occasional occurrences or aberrations. As one SJC member puts it,

You go to the district collector with a request for a water con-nection to the Dalit communities, the fellow will try to help; you go to report a case of social atrocities, he will hit the roof, deny that such cases happen in his jurisdiction, and worse, he will not hesitate to say that you are simply fabricating a case against a high caste person. (personal communication)

These paradoxes of development and democracy emanate from the way the state frames the institutions of local governance. The pursuit of social justice in these proclaimed participa-tory spaces has been premised on two principles—affirmative action to give Dalits entry into panchayat and social inclusion largely through engagement with developmental planning and provisioning. Benefits from development enhance the economic and social status, widen the social space where Dalits interact with upper castes and build confidence among the people who are considered the lowest of the low in caste hierarchy. However, development can seldom address the issues of social justice in totality. Mobilizations, such as Dalit mobilization in Sabarkantha, occasionally stretch the framework when the members bring in to the state sphere radical discourses and practices of social justice. However, the overarching framework of the state prevails.

Mobilization within the state created institutions, therefore, has progressed more in the direction of working with the state. The state–civil society collaboration is considerably reinvented by neoliberalism in the partnership model it popularized, in which the state and civil society are viewed as 'partners' in governance. As the state outsources to civil society not only delivery of services but also the agenda of building democracy, the state and civil society actors are now willing to sit together for deliberation. Within the participatory framework, civil society is assigned the task of doing what the government finds itself unable to do, for instance, dissemination of information in popular language, awareness building and capacity building through training, etc. In short, civil society is expected to enable social groups to be part of local governance programmes. Mobilization involves mediation between the interests of the powerless and those who occupy seats of authority. Therefore, we find that SJCs are adopting negotiation and persuasion as their strategies for social justice.

In this partnership under neoliberalism, which Chandhoke (2003) calls 'pluralization of governance', there is always the danger that the state may control and manipulate civil society, choosing only those civil society actors that it feels comfortable talking to. Hence, while mediation is essential to level the playing field for democratic politics, it has the potential to limit the autonomy of civil society. As the SNM experience suggests, civil society can expand its work within the limited framework of partnership to add momentum to mobilization, but there is a limit to which the framework can be expanded. The SNM, while performing a mediating role, also mobilized Dalits to claim rights and entitlements, yet it had to exercise caution in order to avoid the perception that it is critical of the state or indeed even acting against it. The SNM also realized that their mobilization could only address those rights that the state felt comfortable with or, in a sense, allowed to be part of public discourse. Consequently, talking about the rights of SJC within panchayat system was never perceived as problematic, but talking about the right against social atrocity was.

The local institutions have opened up to Dalit political participation and their ambitions, but have remained largely closed to the substantive inclusion of Dalits as equals, despite tremendous pressure and assertion by Dalit representatives. There are instances of Dalits asserting their political position within the local institutions and bringing a social justice agenda forward for discussion and action within panchayat. However, the institutions themselves have demonstrated their inability and unwillingness to be sufficiently inclusive of Dalit presence or of Dalit voice and interest.

Dalit entry into local government and mobilization by CSOs has resulted in their access to developmental resources, such as housing, water, electricity and roads. This is the most significant gain of Dalit mobilization and has taken care of, to a large extent, the redistribution of material resources and Dalit inclusion in 'development'. The fulfilment of material needs is essential to ensure the upward mobility of Dalits and to enhance their material well-being. In that sense, material needs add value to the Dalit quest for equality and dignity, which are essential elements of social justice. In the absence of equality and inclusion in the social spaces of the wider community and in the political spaces of governance institutions, that quest, however, remains only partially fulfilled.

References

Bardhan, P., and Mukherjee, D. 2000. 'Capture and Governance at Local and National Level'. *The American Economic Review* 90 (2): 135–39.

Chandhoke, N. 2003. 'Governance and Pluralisation: Implications for Democratic Citizenship'. *Economic & Political Weekly* (July 12–18): 2957–68.

Cornwall, A., and Coelho, V. S., eds. 2007. *Spaces for Change? The Politics of Participation in New Democratic Arenas*. London: Zed Books.

Crook, R., and Manor, J. 2000. 'Democratic Decentralization'. OED Working Paper series no. 11. World Bank, Washington, DC.

Crook, R., and Sverisson, A. S. 2001. 'Decentralization and Poverty Alleviation in Developing Countries: A Comparative Analysis or, is West Bengal Unique?' *IDS Working Paper 130*. Institute of Development Studies, Brighton.

Gaventa, J. 2011. 'Towards Participatory Local Governance: Six Propositions for Discussion'. In *The Participation Reader*, edited by A. Cornwall. London: Zed Books.

Government of Gujarat (GoG). 1972. *Zinabhai Darji Committee Report*. Gandhinagar: GoG.

Harriss, J. 2002. *Depoliticizing Development: The World Bank and Social Capital*. London: Anthem Press.

Heller, P. 2001. 'Moving the State: The Politics of Democratic Decentralization in Kerala, South Africa and Porto Alegre'. *Politics and Society* 29 (1): 131–63.

Ilaiah, K. 2001. 'Dalitism and Brahminism: The Epistemological Conflict in History'. In *Dalit Identity and Politics*, edited by G. Shah. New Delhi: SAGE.

Mahajan, G. 1998. *Aspects of Liberal Democracy*. New Delhi: Oxford University Press.

Morris, A., Sharma, A., and Sharma, G. 2008. *Making Spaces: An Enquiry into Women's Participation in Local Politics in Rajasthan*. Study Report, International Development Research Center, Ottawa.

Omvedt, G. 1994. *Dalits and Democratic Revolution*. New Delhi: SAGE.

———. 2001. 'Ambedkar and After: The Dalit movement in India'. In *Dalit Identity and Politics*, edited by G. Shah. New Delhi: SAGE.

Omvedt, G. 2003. 'The Anti-Caste Movement and the Discourse of Power'. In *Democracy in India*, edited by N. G. Jayal. New Delhi: Oxford University Press.

Pai, S. 2002. *Dalit Assertion and the Unfinished Democratic Revolution*. New Delhi: SAGE.

Robinson, M. 2003. 'Participation, Local Governance and Decentralized Service Delivery'. Paper Presented at the Workshop on New Approach to Decentralized Service Delivery: Santiago de Chile, mimeo. Available at www.logolink.org/index.php/respurce/download/534

Satpathy, T. 2006. 'Dalit Leadership in Local Governance'. In *Organising Dalits: Experiences from the Grassroots*, edited by Unnati. Ahmedabad: Unnati.

Shah, G. 1994. 'Politics of Dalit Movement: From Direct Action to Pressure Group'. In *At Crossroads: Dalit Movement Today*, edited by S. Pendse. Mumbai: Vikas Adhyayan Kendra.

———. 2001. 'Dalit Movements and the Search for Identity'. In *Dalit Identity and Politics*. New Delhi: SAGE.

Sumathi, S., and Sudarsen, V. 2005. 'What Does the Panchayat System Guarantee? A Case of Pappapati'. *Economic & Political Weekly*, 3751–58.

Zelliot, E. 2001. *From Untouchable to Dalits: Essays on Ambedkar's Movement*. New Delhi: Manohar Publication.

PHOTO 1: *Protest demonstration in front of the District Collector's Office, Angul, against the land acquisition by Jindal Steel and Power Corporation*

Source: Author.

PHOTO 2: *NREGA workers during lunch break*

Source: Author.

PHOTO 3: *A member of SJC having a discussion in a Dalit settlement, Sabraknatha, Gujarat*

Source: Author.

PHOTO 4: *A meeting of local residents facilitated by Akhil Bharitya Samaj Seva Sansthan, Manikpur, Chitrakoot, Uttar Pradesh*

Source: Author.

PHOTO 5: *The Forest Department of Uttarakhand puts a message warning people against forest destruction*

Source: Author.

PHOTO 6: *The traditional and community-based local water conservation measures initiated by Tarun Bharat Sangh, Alwar, Rajasthan, benefit the farmers*

Source: Author.

5

Joint Forest Management

The Making and Unmaking of Participation

Community participation is an integral part of development projects implemented by the state. Unlike in the 1970s when the notion of participation in development projects was reluctantly accepted under pressure from international aid agencies and voices emanating from the local level, it gained wider acceptance in the 1980s, and, by the mid-1990s, it became mandatory in all development projects. Initially, the participation of people in development was sought with a view to successfully implement projects. With the passage of time, participation became a value to be promoted because including the voice of the marginalized and excluded people in development was thought of as a means of bringing them towards the centre of development.

The formation of village-based institutions is one among many ways of involving people in developmental activities and eliciting their participation. The purpose of forming village level institutions is to provide people ownership of the project. This entails making them an integral part of decision-making, giving them control over their resources and the autonomy to implement the project. Participation is expected to ensure sustainability after the project period is over.

Such institutional spaces have been created by the Indian State at the village level to invite, encourage and enhance participation of the poor, Dalit, tribal groups and women in development. Claiming to be based on democratic principles and procedures, such spaces promise to include the excluded people in deliberations and decision-making in development. The spaces are attractive to people for they promise new way of engagement in development, yet there are caveats, problematics and challenges that characterize their participation.

This chapter discusses VFCs formed under the JFM in Uttaranchal (now Uttarakhand) to engage the village communities in local forest management. It draws from a study the author conducted during 2001–03 in Nainital District.[1] Creating and institutionalizing spaces such as VFCs, the chapter argues, provide necessary, but not sufficient, conditions to ensure the democratization of participation in forest management. It shows how multiple versions of participation coexist within a single institution. Institutional spaces, I argue, are vulnerable to contestations and conflicts of various kinds which means participation does not remain a virtuous normative phenomena, though the normative desirability of participation remains unquestioned.

Cornwall (2002) calls the institutional spaces such as VFCs 'invited spaces' into which people are invited to participate. Unlike created or claimed spaces that people create themselves, the invited spaces are created by external agencies including the state and operate on the basis of predetermined structures

[1] The study was conducted in the villages of Saladi, Soangaon, Jangaliya Gaon, Bannan, Deeni and Parwada in Nainital District, Uttarakhand.

and norms. People sometimes stretch the boundaries of invited spaces, but institutional spaces retain the basic structures and regulations.

The VFCs retain the overall character of invited spaces. However, they also acquire the characteristics of the setting in which they are located and within which they operate. Such spaces are never created in a vacuum; they react upon already existing spaces, on spaces that are simultaneous and overlapping, and they react upon the wider social–economic–cultural setting in which they are embedded. Even when they are created by external agencies, institutional spaces cannot be seen purely as an external or state creation. A certain amount of interest articulation, through overt or covert protest or through deliberation and negotiation, goes into the shaping of these institutional spaces at the micro-level of a village. Such spaces are constantly being created, altered, defined and redefined, with positive promise amidst manipulation, misuse and abuse. Even the most unpromising of institutions may open up possibilities for learning the skills and arts of governance, which people can use in other spaces. Spaces can emerge as arenas of solidarity as well as contestation; they may move between relative openness and closure over time. As such, the chapter suggests that whilst these institutional spaces have the potential to create certain conditions for participation and democracy at the local level, they can also restrict its possibilities, and therefore, must not be conflated either with participation or with democracy.

Shaped by institutional procedures, by actors with affiliations and interests across other spaces, by competing perspectives on forest management and by a variety of forms of participation ranging from formal representation to employment to inclusion in deliberation and decision-making, the dynamics of participation within spaces such as Uttarakhand's VFCs formed under the JFM project was complex. There were practices that treat people as beneficiaries, those that treated them as users/consumers who needed to pay for the services, and there were those that made them citizens with the right to elect their representatives. The practices overlapped and existed simultaneously, and it was this complex intersection of normative ideals and actual practices that influenced participation as was encountered in the villages of Nainital District.

Multiple Spaces in Forest Management

Forests have been an integral part of the lives of people in the Kumaun region of Uttarakhand. People are dependent on forests for a variety of reasons—fuel for cooking, fodder for animals, timber for house construction, medicinal herbs to cure ailments and forest products, such as resin, that have traditionally been source of income. Van panchayat (forest panchayat) was the traditional institutional arrangement for the management of forests. Under the JFM, van panchayats were converted into VFCs. Intersecting with these institutions was gram panchayat, the third tier of the decentralized governance system. These local institutions had a body of elected representatives who constituted the executive committee of a VFC and were responsible for the administrative management of the funds, records and meetings. The executive committees were the centres for decision-making and had control over financial resources.

Regarded locally as the traditional system of forest management, van panchayats were originally created by the colonial administration and retained two essential traditional organizing principles—representation from each hamlet and *mawasa*, a small monetary contribution made by each household to preserve the forest. The foundation was thus laid for the governance of local institutional spaces intended towards participation that were enforceable by law. Resentment raged in the colonial era against state control over forests (Guha 1991). Records from this period reveal that people made claims on the state for the management of forest resources even when the language of rights was unfamiliar to them. The specification of management of forests through van panchayat delineated the content and boundaries of local action—what people were granted and allowed to claim and what they were not granted, and therefore, were barred from. This not only restricted the local institutional management of forest to the civil forest and limited access to the reserved forests, but it also specified what kind of actions were to be allowed in the institutional spaces for local participation in forest management.

These institutions have persisted even in post-independent India. The patterns established during the colonial regime have remained unchecked, such as the practices that inhibited, if not purposefully restricted, the participation of certain social groups, such as women as voters, members or even as participants in the village meetings. The joint management of forest resources under the Village JFM Rules, 1997, attempted to make village communities participants in forest management. It also attempted to forge a collaborative relationship between the state and village communities. Yet the very basis of these institutional spaces situated, and continues to situate, the state as giver of rights and the owner of the forest and the people as manager of only those areas that the state allows.

Changing Perspectives on Forest Management and Institutional Changes

In earlier times, before the establishment of the colonial regime, forests were managed by people as a common property resource. Through a variety of social and cultural sanctions, the hill people combined their subsistence-related dependency on nature with its conservation. By dedicating the hilltops to the local deities, people were made to venerate forests. Informal institutions of management were also in place to protect the forests, for instance, in the oak forests, there were informal rules that prohibited the lopping off leaves during summer months. These rules also specified, according to the need of each household, the amount of grass to be cut by each family. Those who violated these rules were subjected to social sanctions and were often denied entry into forests. People were required to pay the king for medicinal herbs and other forest produces that were commercially exploited, but, as far as the access to and use of forests were concerned, there were hardly any restrictions imposed by the kings (Guha 1991).

All this changed with the establishment of colonial administration in Kumaun. The forest management and institutional arrangements in British Kumaun not only restricted people's access to and use of the forest, it also created formal institutions to regulate them. The British administration's interest in the forests was guided by two factors—supply of timber to build railway tracks and war ships and the supply of fuel to the administrative centres in Nainital, Almora and the cantonment town of Ranikhet. Between 1815 and 1917, the British administration brought forests under state control, and large patches of forests were declared 'reserved' under the 1878 Indian Forest Act. The state control of forests regulated and restricted the access to and use of forests by people and there was resistance against the measures taken up by the British Administration (Guha 1991). As a result, the British Administration decided to grant some control to local communities on the less commercially viable patches. Van panchayats[2] were created in 1931 under the Kumaun Panchayat Forest Rules, 1931 (amended in 1976 and further amended in 2001). The revenue department was given the responsibility of forming a van panchayat in a village if one-third of its residents put in an application for its formation. The forest department was given the responsibility of providing technical guidance to van panchayats.

Van panchayat members are elected in an open meeting that is attended by all the adult residents of the village; they then select the sarpanch, who is the head of the van panchayat. Each hamlet called *tok* has at least one representative in the

[2] For government rules and regulation by which van panchayats are guided, see GoUP (1976) and GoU (2001).

van panchayat. A van panchayat usually has from five to nine members and is given the responsibility of plantation and regeneration of forests, management of the *panchayati*[3] forests, appointment of a watchman for the protection of forests and levying of fines on offenders. The van panchayat fund built out of the sale of forest produce, such as timber, resin, etc., is deposited with the deputy commissioner at Nainital.

Until 1947, the chief motive of the state's control over the forests and limited rights to people was guided by the commercial exploitation of forests to serve the British administration. After independence, the motive became revenue generation. The path to economic development made forests a prime target for scientific management and control (Gadgil and Guha 1992). The state control over forests gave rise to contestations between the users of forests and the state (Pathak 1994).

The situation began to change in the late 1980s when state control over the forests came under criticism; when it was realized that the alienation of village communities from the forests had significantly damaged the forests and that people needed to be brought into the management of forests in a more active way. These shifts in forest management reflected the shift in the development discourse to accommodate people's participation. This shift required changes in the institutional arrangement for forest management as well as in the orientation of the forest bureaucracy. Instead of concentrating on the commercial worth of forests, they were required to emphasize on the subsistence needs of the people and ecological considerations. Instead of taking the entire responsibility for the management of forests, they were required to share it with the local communities.

The National Forest Policy of India, 1988, the Uttar Pradesh State Forest Policy, 1996 (earlier, Uttarakhand was a part of Uttar Pradesh), the Uttarakhand Forest Policy, 2001, and the Village JFM Rules, 1997, laid emphasis on participatory forest management. These policy resolutions tried to constitute the

[3] Village forests that belong to panchayats.

local institutions on the principles of democracy rather than on the colonial conception of control. Participatory democracy and development require that people, who are dependent on forests for their subsistence, get a stake in its management, not because the state is pleased to grant them that stake, but because that is the way democracy and development must function. In this normative version of participation, participation is sought not to fulfil some ulterior motives of the state, that is, to minimize the voice of resistance or prevent encroachment on commercially viable forests, but to integrate the marginalized and the excluded into the process of development. Nevertheless, an undertone of power and restrictions associated with the state-given rights can be discerned in the functioning of the village institutions and the language of the foresters.

The Village JFM Rules 1997 provided administrative basis to the JFM and further reinvigorated village institutional space. It specified VFCs as forum for local participation in forest management, and VFCs were to be created by either converting the van panchayats or as subcommittee of gram panchayat. The usual practice in Kumaun has been to convert the van panchayats into VFCs. The Uttarakhand Forest Policy, 2001, gave primacy to ecological considerations and community participation over commercial valuation of forests. The policy lays special consideration for women's participation in forest management.

The World Bank assisted JFM project converted the existing van panchayats into VFCs for a period of four years during which the project was implemented. The van panchayats (turned into VFCs) were thus given the responsibility of the preparation of micro-plan for the project activities, taking steps to protect the forests, distributing the forest products equitably, undertaking new plantation and working towards forest regeneration. While the van panchayat funds were deposited with the deputy commissioner, JFM funds were utilized directly by the VFCs. The sarpanch of the VFC and the forest guard from the forest department were given the joint responsibility to utilize the financial resources. Besides, each VFC built a village development fund (VDF). While the JFM provided VFCs with the financial resources to implement the project, it also demanded that people contribute to the cost of the project. It thus became the responsibility of a VFC to seek contributions from village households. Part of this contribution came in the form of labour whereby either people contributed free labour for JFM-related activities and the wages are deposited in the VDF or they contributed part of their wages to the fund. Under the JFM, the VFCs, in addition to the *panchayati* forests, were given the responsibility of managing patches of the reserved forests close to the village, thus bringing, for the first time in the history of forest management, the state-controlled reserved forests under the joint management of the people and the forest department. The limited space of van panchayats, when turned into VFCs, got expanded, altered and filled with new activities, new skills and new ways of participation.

VFC: Dynamics of Participation in Forest Management

The dynamics of participation taking place within the VFCs can be analysed through five variables: actors occupying the institutional space of the VFC and their influence; competing knowledge/perspectives on forest management; varieties of participation and the nature of engagement taking place within the VFCs; institutional procedures guiding the VFCs and the management of resources, particularly financial resources and their allocation for forest management; and village politics and the nature of participation.

Actors and Influence

Of all the actors, the state is the most influential in the arena of forest management. Comprised as it is of heterogeneous, sometimes competing, institutions, the state nonetheless has a central character, which is more overpowering and pervasive than the fragmentations and conflicts among those who represent it. The role the state has played in the history of forest management has vested it with immense power. There were many occasions when I found people unhappy with the way the forest department and the revenue department manage JFM, yet with a strong belief that the JFM project as well as the VFC as an institution are inherently beneficial, and that in places where good officers are in charge, the project had delivered the desired goods. The mismanagement and authoritarianism of the government agencies were considered merely an anomaly or a reflection of the idiosyncrasies of specific officers.

Although JFM was said to be based on the principles of participation and shared responsibilities, in reality, the forest department simply carved out a bigger role for itself and made the VFC dependent on it for the planning and inflow of finances. The forest guard, as the member-secretary of the VFC, had the power to operate the JFM bank account jointly with the sarpanch. The control therefore still rested with the forest department. In the village of Soangaon, financial embezzlement by the forest guard led to distrust in the VFC, and the VFC was eventually stalled by the forest department. Soangaon perhaps is an extreme example, but the lack of autonomy in planning and financial matters made many VFCs disinterested in taking responsibilities for forest management.

The local institutional space is the locus of power and can patronize those that enjoy the decision-making powers in these institutions. As they are close allies of the state, the power of the state is transmitted to and through them to the institutional space. This power is manifested in being able to manage finances, write reports, maintain accounts, organize meetings and distribute work. In the case of the JFM, decisions were often taken in closed-door meetings, or they were taken with the forest guard and the divisional forest officer (DFO) and later approved in village meetings. The sarpanch or the influential members in VFCs tried to do maximum work related to plantation in their own *tok*.

Below this layer came people who held other forms of status, whether from their social standing, such as teachers, or ex-sarpanchs, and from their caste and economic position, or as a result of political lobbying. The influence these actors exerted was both positive and negative. They gave direction to decision-makers and could counterbalance the state interference, but they also had the potential to exercise their own influence to exploit forests and alienate the needy from forest management.

At the end of the spectrum came the people who were most dependent on forests. They held the least political power, had no social standing, particularly, if they belonged to lower castes, and were vulnerable and alienated from the public space if they were women. This category was the most vulnerable to external influence coming from the state or others in the village. However, they were not completely powerless. While others exercised a lot of visible power, this category had its own ways of resistance and dealing with the powerful. One of the potent methods of resistance was refusal to provide labour. Since most of them were wage labourers, their refusal sent the signal of resistance. This refusal did not paralyse the employer so much economically as it did politically, because the opponents either voluntarily sought the patronage of the rival fraction or were invited to join them. Gossip remained another form of resistance. Gossip often centred around the misappropriation of funds by the sarpanch or other members of the panchayat. These 'weapons of the weak' and 'hidden transcripts' (Scott 1990) turned spaces for participation into arenas of contestation rather than solidarity and warmth. The more people remained outside the institutional spaces, the more exclusionary the spaces became.

Competing Knowledge and Perspectives

It may sound paradoxical that people could also resent control by the same state that they otherwise venerate. But historical evidence reveals resentment against the extension of state control over forests during different periods.[4] As mentioned earlier, the colonial period witnessed violent protests against the British Administration when it tried to alienate people from the forests. Subsequently, resentment centred on the overwhelming presence of the revenue department in local village forest management, its strict control over van panchayat funds and the high-handedness of forest guards. Under the JFM, part of the reserved forest came within the purview of the VFCs. But people knew that once the project period was over, it would return to the control of the forest department. Even the ownership and control of local forests, the management of which rested with van panchayats, was under the revenue department. This turned people into mere managers of forests owned by the state, and resentment against the state simmered.

Negation of the 'willingness to manage' forests in favour of the 'technical expertise to manage' became more pervasive under the JFM. Fund management, accounts keeping and, above all understanding the technicalities and complexities of the project-favoured people who were literate. Hence, in spite of the supposedly good principles of participation, which JFM advocated, in reality discriminated those who were illiterate although knowledgeable about the forests. There was hardly any scope within the project frame to accommodate people who could not understand the technicalities of the project but who were bestowed with local wisdom, willingness, commitment and spontaneity to look after their forest resources.

Dimensions of Participation

In the precolonial period, abundant forests and low population pressure left the access to forest resources relatively unfettered.

---

[4] I have already cited the protest during the British administration. After independence, the Chipko Movement, particularly by women in the hills of Uttarakhand, who resisted the commercial felling of trees by hugging them, revealed the tenuous relationship between the people and the state in matters related to the use and control of forests (see Bhatt 1991; Guha 1991).

By turning the forest into a commercially viable resource, the colonial state restricted people's engagement with the management of forest resources. The constitution of van panchayats and the recognition of certain rights over the forest gave participation a formal, legal and institutional shape. Participation of the people thereafter was confined to voting in the elections of van panchayat and abiding by the rules that governed the *panchayati* forest. In this system of forest management, women seldom participated, either as voters or as members of the panchayat committee, and they seldom attended panchayat meetings. Many van panchayats became defunct over the years due to lack of funds, lack of interest by the revenue and forest departments and due to unresolved village conflicts. The JFM gave the van panchayats a new lease of life as VFCs. Yet participation in and through the VFCs remained limited.

Poor people's participation in forest management under the JFM had been synonymous with employment. The JFM, following the general pattern of development projects, emphasized contributions to the project in the form of labour. A certain percentage of wages were deposited in the VDF, supposedly, to promote a sense of ownership among people. In an economic setting with few employment opportunities, project work such as plantation, check-dam construction, etc., were sought after by the poor. People cited the period of project-related employment as the time when attendance for meeting was larger and more regular than at any other time.

Given economic realities, the project work did help poor people, but their sense of involvement like their employment in the project remained temporary. Hence, once the project was completed, there was little further involvement. Since their involvement in the project and their understanding of the role of the VFC remained inadequate, their sense of ownership of the project lasted until the completion of the project. In fact, and ironically so, a large number of people whose contribution had gone to build the village fund were not even aware that a portion of their wages was kept in the fund.

The JFM projectized participation and turned it into employment, and the state continued to hold regulatory power over the VFCs. The instrumentalities of participation were not abandoned completely. But limited as these participatory spaces were, there is also no denying that they created opportunities for the marginalized groups to play a part in decision-making. So even if the landscape of marginalization was not completely altered, new leadership emerged from the poor and the marginalized social groups of women and Dalits. By acquainting people with the language of the state and state-led rules, the JFM taught people the art of governance, no matter how rudimentary that was.

Institutional Procedures

The supervisory and regulatory procedures of the state affected participation in many ways. Under the JFM, the VFCs were superimposed on van panchayats. The lack of coordination between the two government departments responsible for the formation of these institutions and their supervision filled the space with conflicts. Although existing van panchayats were converted into VFCs, the VFCs were not allowed to utilize the van panchayat fund during the JFM project period. This restricted their activities as the JFM funds could be spent only on activities mentioned in the micro-plan of the project. While the VFCs largely had to work with the forest department, the responsibility of VFC elections still rested with the revenue department. The lack of departmental co-ordination had implications for the functioning of VFCs.

Village Politics and the Nature of Participation

As a representative body of people, the VFC signified people's participation. But, alongside that, it was required to seek wider participation and engagement of the people. The provision for the reservation of seats for Dalits and women gave them a formal place in the decision-making forum of the VFC. The nature and extent of participation, however, remained contingent on the power between social groups as well as power between the VFC as an institution and the village community. This shaped the nature of participation: Participation became both inclusive and exclusive, and also both open and closed.

This aspect is discussed elaborately in the next section.

Local Context, Village Dynamics and the Nature of Participatory Spaces: Exclusion and Inclusion in Forest Management

This section discusses village micro contexts that influence the nature of participation.

Deeni was predominantly inhabited by lower castes. In terms of their economic standing, the majority of people had small landholdings. There were also a few households that did not possess any land. A few families who were better off had migrated to the cities and nearby towns. Cultivation was the main livelihood of the village. The village had many households earning their livelihood as skilled labour. Deeni residents were highly dependent on forests for fuel and fodder. Despite being closer to a town and connected by roads, they could not afford to use Liquefied Petroleum Gas (LPG) fuel for cooking. As a result, women travelled long distances every day to get wood from the forests.

Deeni had no history of women participating in van panchayats. It was only when the VFC was formed that they entered into the public spaces of deliberation and decision-making. Instrumental in opening up the space for them was the active interest taken by the VFC sarpanch and the DFO. Backed and supported by the DFO and other members of the VFC, the sarpanch not only recruited women to the VFC but also mobilized them to take part in the deliberations of the VFCs and entrusted them with the task of protecting the forests so that they could also have some extra income. During our discussions, women felt comfortable in expressing their views openly. There was no overt aggression or intolerance shown by the male members.

In Deeni, people were happy with the way the sarpanch and the VFC members had taken care to divide the project-related employment opportunities equitably among people. There were no allegations of favouring particular families or a particular *tok*. The VFC earned the respect and trust of people because the accounts were kept open, and there was transparency in managing the JFM and the VFC fund. The VFC in Deeni shared a cordial relationship with the gram panchayat. All this contributed in making the institutional space open, visible and inclusive, and there was an atmosphere of trust and solidarity.

Contrast this with Bannan that was predominantly inhabited by upper castes with a very sharp economic division among people. There were a few affluent families, but a sizable number of families were either without any landholdings or owned small landholdings. They worked as labourers to earn their livelihood. Agriculture was the main source of livelihood. For the landless families working as labourers, agriculture provided the main form of employment except, occasionally, when the construction of a school or road provided them work. People, particularly the economically needy, were highly dependent on forests for fodder and fuel. Women travelled long distances to collect these from forests. Bannan too had no history of women participation in van panchayat. This exclusionary aspect persisted, and the VFC thus lacked any female membership. While talking to women, it became apparent that they did not have much information about the JFM. The only event most of them remembered was when they attended a village meeting to discuss the micro planning for the project. Subsequently, they were seldom called for any meeting except for those that were called to provide them temporary employment in the JFM project.

It was not surprising then that people associated the JFM with the employment it provided. As no effort was taken either by the VFC or by the forest officials to make their inclusion substantive, they remained unaware of the larger purpose of the project and participation in forest management. Not only did people in the village accuse the sarpanch and the VFC members of favouring people from their own *tok* in matters of distribution of project-related work, there was also distrust regarding the management of the JFM fund and the VDF. In people's perception, the forest department appeared as a disinterested actor, seldom visiting the village and not having any interest in settling the conflicts, distrust and disagreement which had affected the VFC.

The VFC and the gram panchayats were at loggerheads and as a consequence, the entire village was divided into factions. The gram pradhan, who was the wife of the previous pradhan, and comes from a relatively affluent family, had been instrumental in alienating the VFC. Before the JFM was introduced in Bannan, the Swajal Project, a water and sanitation project of the World Bank, was implemented in the village. The pradhan was the chief functionary in the village entrusted with the responsibility of implementing the project. That gave her enormous power within the village as well as the opportunity to gain the support and trust of the people. She felt left out and also somewhat threatened when the JFM was introduced in the village and the van panchayat sarpanch became powerful. She lodged a false complaint against the sarpanch of misappropriating the fund. As a result, the project was stalled in Bannan for a period of time.

A variant of the conflict-ridden spaces was Soangaon, where the conflict was largely fuelled by factionalism in the village and a biased forest department. Soangaon was inhabited by upper castes with only a few families from the lower castes, who lived in a separate hamlet quite far away from the village. A large number of people in the village were employed in nearby towns, for example, Bhimtal—the tourist town was close to the village and provided employment opportunities to the villagers. As a result, the dependency on forests was relatively less. Before the JFM was introduced in the village, the van panchayat was inactive. Some powerful people from the village were known to be engaged in illegal encroachment of forests, but the van panchayat was indifferent to it. The members were either employed in government jobs or running their own private business, too busy to devote any time to the management of forests. When the JFM was introduced, some members continued with their usual indifferent attitude. However, with huge sums of money coming from the JFM, the situation could not remain the same. The powerful groups in the village lobbied against the VFC. The VFC could not show them the exact expenditure incurred by it. People suspected that the forest guard, taking advantage of the trust of the sarpanch, who was a government employee, and therefore, could not devote much time to the VFC, misappropriated the fund. The forest department did not try to investigate the matter further displaying favouritism towards its own department personnel and withdrew the JFM project from Soangaon.

The people, who had lobbied against the VFC, formed a new VFC with the ex-gram pradhan as its head. The general opinion of the villagers was that the new VFC, rather than having any real interest in the forests, was more interested in managing the fund. However, the forest department by that time had already decided to withdraw the project and the new VFC remained only a transient formation. Talking to people in Soangaon, it became apparent that they were hardly interested in forest management. Forests seemed important only to a few lower caste and poor families, as they were dependent on it. Yet, the conflicts that ensued in the village among the powerful left these forest dependent families outside the periphery of any decision-making. As a result, the spaces created for participation remained closed and almost non-existent.

From the instance of a village, where the spaces for participation was open and visible, and two instances where they were closed and conflict ridden, the discussion now moves to villages where the spaces were a mix of both open and closed, visible and inclusive, and sites of occasional conflict and contestation.

Saladi was inhabited by the upper castes. People earned their livelihood through agriculture and employment in government and private jobs in nearby towns. A few families worked as wage labourers. As Saladi is close to the main road, people could easily get LPG fuel for cooking. However, since many families were not in an economically sound position to afford LPG on a continuous basis, they had to collect wood for fuel from the forests. They were also dependent on the forests for fodder for their cattle. Like Deeni, the women were given a chance to be in the VFC due to the efforts of the sarpanch and the forest officials. The sarpanch had also recruited women in the safety squads for the protection of the forests. I found the women vocal and articulate. The women VFC members were quite active. They were aware of forest-related issues, had information about the project, and were not inhibited to talk in the public. The relationship between the VFC and the gram panchayat was of occasional solidarity, but there was rivalry beneath this solidarity. People trusted the VFC for its openness in dealing with the JFM the VDF funds. However, there was competition among women for employment in the project activities which occasionally turned into conflict. The sarpanch tried to employ women on a rotational basis, but unlike Deeni where women were comfortable with this arrangement, women in Saladi at times accused the VFC of favouring certain families. This sense of being discriminated, actual or perceived, resulted in occasional distrust and anomaly.

Parwada was predominantly inhabited by the upper castes with a few lower caste families living in a separate hamlet. A few families in the village owned large landholdings and were engaged in cash cropping. The remaining households either held small landholdings or were landless. The village was known for illegal encroachment of forests by the affluent sections. There was a high dependency of the poor families on the forests for fodder and fuel. Parwada had a history of active involvement of women in the public sphere as members of the Mahila Mangal Dal (Women Welfare Group), women's collectives formed to integrate them with various state-led developmental interventions. The van panchayat, which was later converted into the VFC, also had a woman sarpanch. This made participation quite open until conflict ensued between people who were influential and illegal encroachers of forests and the VFC. The influential section resented the VFC due to its strict measures, and the sarpanch being a woman further added to their resentment. They lodged a complaint against the VFC that it had become too high handed and that fresh elections should be held to settle the conflict. The nexus between the revenue department and the powerful people in Parwada on the one hand, and the rivalry between the revenue department and the forest department on the other, resulted in the formation of an interim VFC. All these factors in various measures contributed in shaping the participatory spaces—the spaces that were once open became fragmented and were filled with distrust and conflict.

In Jangalia Gaon, the spaces for participation were largely open, visible but insufficiently inclusive, and were filled with occasional distrust. The village was inhabited by the upper castes. There was high dependency on the forests for fodder and fuel. Like Parwada, in Jangalia Gaon too, women had been quite active in forestry-related issues due to the efforts of a local organization called CHIRAG (Central Himalayan Rural Action Group) that mobilized women to form the Van Suraksha Samitis (Forest Protection Committees; women's collectives formed for afforestation activities). As a result, women began raising saplings and protecting the forests. However, despite this active engagement, the VFC did not include women as members. The VFC did not discriminate against them, but did not take an active interest in integrating them either. Women, nonetheless, attended the VFC meetings. The VFC was open in its decision-making, but occasionally it lacked transparency in managing the finances of the project. This gave rise to suspicion among the people that got accentuated due to the late payment of wages to those employed in the project. While the VFC was constrained due to the late disbursement of fund from the JFM, people suspected the VFC for the misappropriation of the fund.

The VFC in Jangalia Gaon enjoyed the support of the gram panchayat. As a result, it did not face any opposition in the village. Since the pradhan was a woman, women were also encouraged to take interest in the JFM-related activities, but were frustrated that they were not included as members in the VFC.

Presence, Influence and Voice: Women in JFM

To what extent, then, does a project like the JFM actually extend the new opportunities for involvement and the voice of the more marginalized actors as it promised? What did participation actually come to mean? And how did less vocal people, such as women, engage with the spaces for participation that village institutions made available? Taking the case of women's participation, some of the paradoxes of participation in JFM become evident.

Talking to women in the hilly villages of Uttarakhand revealed the tension that underlined their trying to break with the status quo. One woman from Jangalia Gaon spoke for many when she said, 'It is like a risky walk on the rope. We do not want to displease the male members, but at the same time we do not want to lose out on the opportunity of coming out of the house and being part of the processes taking place in the village'. Is there any backlash they face? 'Yes, sometimes, but gradually and also due to the constant encouragement of the DFO *saab*, things have improved' (personal communication).

The JFM made it mandatory that certain percentage of women must be present in the VFC. In practice, however, the inclusion of women often became dependent on government officials and the sarpanch. In Deeni and Saladi, women got membership in the VFC because the forest officials as well as the sarpanchs were keen on including them. Women's inclusion thus depended to a large extent on the goodwill of men, whether they were VFC heads, who were usually male, and forest bureaucracy, also usually male. It would be erroneous, however, to conclude that women could have stood better chance of inclusion in VFC if the sarpanchs were women. The woman sarpanch of Jangalia Gaon did not include women in VFC despite women being very active in forest protection. The marginal space for women's participation shrank further when the institutions became conflict ridden and closed as happened in Bannan, Parwada and Soangaon.

Even when women found a place in the decision-making body, they seldom spoke. The mere presence of women in decision-making spaces did not guarantee that their voices would be raised, heard or have an impact. It is naïve to expect that spaces which had hitherto remained exclusive would open up and become inclusive by merely giving women a formal place. The reason for women not being able to speak or their voices not being heard are many: cultural barriers of not speaking in front of elderly male members of the family or the village and the patriarchal system in which women seldom occupy public space or are even recognized as capable of taking a public decision.[5] As Ganga Joshi from CHIRAG reflected,

> It is much easier to organize women's collectives where they can speak uninhibited. But then that is not what women's participation in the long run should look like. If they have to be integrated into the wider process, we have to face the challenge of enabling them to speak in a forum which is not exclusively for women. (personal communication)

Women were complacent, arguing that whatever decision their fathers, husbands or other male members in the family or village ask them to take would eventually prove beneficial. This hides the critical and dangerous consequence that their mere presence without voice can be used to legitimize decisions.

---

[5] Citing the case of women's participation in the VFC in Gonduru village in Uttar Kannada, Sunder et al. (2001, 114) write, 'as a "daughter of the village" she could voice her opinion, but once she became a "daughter-in-law of the village", moreover, one married into the chairperson's household, her freedom to speak in front of family and village elders was severely curtailed'.

Without much of a presence or voice in decision-making arenas, village women were expected to participate in public meetings related to local forest management. Due to usual household work, which included among other things collection of fuel and fodder and assisting men with farm activities, time was scarce for women. The arena in which women were found to be most active was in implementation, yet their predominance here raises concerns about issues of equity and about the relationship between the spaces of participation in implementation and those in which management decisions are taken. Women were often employed as members of the safety squad to guard the forests against illegal lopping or encroachment. Though it helped them earn extra income for the family it also burdened them. They had to patrol the forests at night, which meant there was hardly any time left for them to rest. While the entire household benefited from the forest resources, men took all the important decisions regarding forests and women continued to take the burden of their protection. And while women faced daily harassment from the forest officials, and found many ways to negotiate with them, when it came to decision-making regarding forest management issues, they were systematically pushed to the margins.

Other spaces in which women can gain confidence, skills and a sense of their own capabilities prove significant in enabling women to engage in forest management activities (Agarwal 1997). During the JFM project period, women's participation was enhanced in those villages where there was an already existent forum and space for women created either by voluntary organizations, such as CHIRAG, in the form of Van Suraksha Samiti or by the government in the form of Mahila Mangal Dal. These other spaces invariably remained outside the spaces created by the government exclusively for the purpose of forest management.

Where women were linked in a sustained and integrated manner with the project as in the villages of Saladi and Deeni, new leadership emerged from among women. With it emerged newfound confidence that was visible in many ways—in meetings, in articulating issues and in dealing with the project authorities. The involvement of women enhanced the quality of participation. The spaces that were denied to women became more open and participatory, though they remained restrictive given women's existing workload.

The dynamic interplay of power between institutions responsible for the promotion of participation as well as between institutions and people turns the spaces into negotiating fields and participation in forest management into an essentially political act. Who comes into the space, who takes decisions, whose voice counts, who is left at the margins, then, depends not only on how power operates in that particular space but also on how it operates between different state institutions, between the state and people, among various groups in the village having differential positioning in the society and among groups having different institutional affiliations. In this process of negotiation, there is always the possibility of the marginalized vulnerable sections being excluded from decision-making.

Given their transformatory nature, the conflicts and contestations which fill them and the power dynamics which influence them, these spaces remain complex and contested. Necessary, but not sufficient to foster participation, however open these spaces may be, they need to be constantly guarded, particularly by those who are the most vulnerable and are more likely than others to be left at the margin.

References

Agarwal, B. 1997. 'Re-sounding the Alert: Gender, Resources and Community Action'. World Development 25: 1373–80.

Bhatt, C. P. 1991. 'Chipko Movement: The Hug that Saves'. Survey of the Environment, The Hindu, 17–23.

Cornwall, A. 2002. 'Making Spaces, Changing Spaces: Situating Participation in Development'. Working Paper no. 170 Institute of Development Studies, Brighton.

Gadgil, M., and Guha, R. 1992. The Fissured Land: An Ecological History of India. New Delhi: Oxford University Press.

Gaventa, J., Shankland, A., and Howard, J. 2002. 'Making Rights Real: Exploring Citizenship, Participation and Accountability'. *IDS Bulletin* 33 (2): 1–14.

Government of Uttar Pradesh (GoUP). 1976. *Van Panchayat* Rules (Hindi). Lucknow: Forest and Wildlife Department, GoUP.

Government of Uttar Pradesh (GoUP). 1998. *Joint Forest Management Guidelines* (Hindi). Lucknow: Forest Department, GoUP.

Government of Uttarakhand (GoU). 2001. *The Uttaranchal Panchayati Forest Rules*. Dehradun: Forest Department, GoU.

Guha, R. 1991. *The Unquiet Woods: Ecological Change and Peasant Resistance in the Himalaya*. New Delhi: Oxford University Press.

Pathak, A. 1994. *Contested Domains: The State, Peasants and Forests in Contemporary India*. New Delhi: SAGE.

Scott, J. 1990. *Dominance and the Arts of Resistance: Hidden Transcripts*. New Haven, CT: Yale University Press.

Sunder, N., Jeffry, R., and Thin, N. 2001. *Branching Out: Joint Forest Management in India*. New Delhi: Oxford University Press.

6

The Kol Resistance
Tribal Mobilization for Land Rights

Land is a highly valuable asset in an agrarian economy. Land is a symbol of both economic and social power for those who possess large landholdings. For those who are part of the subsistence economy, land is not only a means for agriculture and food production, but is also the most basic resource that ensures other resources such as water and forest. There are two broad streams through which poor people's land claims have been articulated in India: (a) saving land from industrial encroachment that takes away private land under land acquisition legislations for public good; and (b) claiming land as distributive justice—this claim comes from the land reforms in the 1950s–70s that promised land to the landless and the poor farmers. Distributive justice is invoked in recent times in claiming homestead land for the homeless and agricultural land for the landless.[1] This chapter addresses the land claims that followed the land reforms.

[1] Ekta Parishad, a CSO based in Madhya Pradesh, is spearheading the claim for homestead land and land to the landless.

The land reforms initiated in the 1950s were considered radical policy initiatives to reform the agriculture sector to enhance production as well as to bridge the inequality in rural areas by distributing land to the poorest of the poor—the landless, agricultural worker, marginal farmer, SC and ST. The land reforms in Uttar Pradesh had promised agricultural land, most of it ceiling surplus land recovered from the landed households through the new land reforms legislations vested in gram sabha to be distributed free of cost to the poorest. The Kol Tribals living in Chitrakoot District of Uttar Pradesh, one of the poorest group of people, however, could not benefit from the land reforms as the land distribution was marred by the landed upper caste and their nexus with the administration. The Kols, many of them poor, landless and serving as bonded labour to the landed upper castes at that time, could not fight against their masters/employers. It is in this situation that Akhil Bharatiya Samaj Seva Sansthan (ABSSS), a grassroots organization based in Chitrakoot, mobilized the Kols and took them on a path of resistance which was both resisting the oppression as well as asserting their rights. It organized the Kols to demand land distribution even as it sought to free them from bondage. The chapter discusses the Kol mobilization for land rights and the role of a CSO in bringing democracy and development to one of the poorest and most marginalized sections.

Chitrakoot District is located in the Bundelkhand region, which is one of the most socio-economically backward regions in the country. The region has seen periodic droughts and hunger deaths, including suicide committed by farmers due to poverty, crop failure and growing indebtedness. It was in this region that ABSSS mobilized the Kols to fight for their rights, resist exploitation, pursue self-reliance in livelihoods and reconstruct social relationships. Working within the Gandhian principles of non-violent struggle and rural reconstruction, ABSSS has extended the right-based framework to address issues of social justice and economic development of the marginalized sections in Bundelkhand. ABSSS worked through a multi-pronged strategy of social mobilization based on collectivization of the Kols, advocacy campaigns, legal action, direct interaction with the government agencies and support in promoting self-reliance in people to build their ecosystem of resources and livelihoods.

The Kol mobilization put in the larger context of development and social justice indicates the following.

1. Struggle to access development, in this case a piece of land, is not an isolated struggle. How do people, who are in bondage, own land? How do they get recognized as citizens with rights?
2. Social and economic justices are intertwined, and social justice, freedom from bondage in this case, is a pre-condition of economic development. The release from bondage was essential for people to claim land rights.
3. Possession of a small piece of agricultural land, not even an acre in many cases, and in many cases, uncultivable due to poor soil quality, does not drastically change the economic inequalities. What value do people see in land ownership that inspires them to struggle hard to get possession of the land? What does the long struggle for a small patch of land mean to those who have been in bondage to the landed?
4. In highly unequal and exploitative social and economic settings, the struggle for rights is long and arduous. Big gains are few and far between, but there are small and incremental gains that strengthen the collectives, empower them and keep the struggle alive. That the Kols could ask questions to a district collector when he travelled through their villages is by no means an insignificant gain for them.
5. External support, in this case ABSSS, plays a critical role where people trapped in entrenched inequalities find it difficult to pitch themselves against the powerful in society and the state apparatus on their own.

Land Reforms

The First Five Year Plan (1951–56) put land reforms at the centre of development. Land reforms were designed to reform the agriculture sector, boost agriculture productivity, eradicate poverty, reduce inequalities in land ownership and promote social justice by distributing land to the landless and marginal farmers. Land reforms were aimed at the abolition of the zamindari system and rent collectors, reform of land tenure system, imposition of land ceiling on those who had excess land, and consolidation of landholdings. The surplus land collected through ceiling was vested in gram sabhas along with other kinds of land, and was to be distributed to the rural poor.

The states were to formulate and implement their own land reform legislations following the guidelines from the central government. While the land reforms removed the intermediaries and reformed old modes of production, the redistribution of land to the poor lagged behind. Further, while the reforms had a positive impact on agriculture and poverty, they could not address the issues of inequality in land ownership in rural areas (Besley and Burgess 2000). Many landowners surrendered land but only inferior and uncultivable land. In many cases, those who had received land could not make proper use of the land as they did not have the money to improve the soil (Planning Commission).

Uttar Pradesh passed three sets of land legislations as part of land reforms—Zamindari Abolition and Land Reforms Act, 1950; Imposition of Ceilings on Landholdings Act, 1960; and Consolidation of Landholdings Act, 1953. In 1972, the central government issued guidelines specifying the land ceiling limits: (a) the best land, 10 acres, (b) for second-class land, 18–27 acres; and (c) for the rest, 27–54 acres with a slightly higher limit in the hill and desert areas.

Uttar Pradesh was successful in the possession and allotment of surplus land to the landless.

By the year 1985, in Uttar Pradesh 2800 acres of land had been found surplus and out of this nearly 1570 acres of land had been allotted to landless cultivators up to the end of 30th June, 1986 and the remaining land was supposed to be distributed in the year 1986–87. By the year 2005, out of 366147 acres of land declared surplus, 335525 acres were under the possession of government. (Vachhani et al. 2009, 59)

The ceiling surplus land was vested with the gram sabha and was to be managed and distributed by the Land Management Committee of panchayat institutions that were formed under the Uttar Pradesh Panchayat Act, 1947. Each panchayat was to keep the records of cultivable area, yield per year as well as a land record map.

However, while land titles were issued, the actual possession of land remained difficult, and it took a long time for the beneficiaries to own the land allotted to them. A study (Vachhani et al. 2009) in 10 districts of Uttar Pradesh shows that a majority of beneficiaries of ceiling surplus land have been landless agriculture workers and belong to SCs. In many cases, the land allotted is of bad quality, non-irrigable, and without any irrigation facilities. The size of the landholdings in many cases is below one acre. However, a majority of households cultivate the land they have received as part of land reforms even though the yield is meagre. While the yield does not contribute significantly to household income, the land ownership has decreased the wage income. Besides, the farmers have been able to avail institutional credit for cultivation. In Chitrakoot District, the actual possession of land became difficult as big landholders, who belong to the upper caste, used their alliance with the local bureaucracy, police and politicians to obstruct the process (Joshi 2003). Furthermore, some families lost the ceiling land that was given to them as the forest department disposed them from the land and turned the land into reserve forest (FIAN 2004).

At the same time as the government initiated land reforms to take surplus land from big landholders and distribute among the landless, Vinoba Bhave, a Gandhian social reformer, began the Bhoodan Movement asking people to donate land voluntarily. The Bhoodan Movement began on 18 April 1951 in Pochampally village, Nalgonda, in Andhra Pradesh. Bhave travelled across the country by foot for close to a decade asking people to donate their excess land. As a result of his relentless work, over 4 million acres of land was given away as voluntary donations to be distributed to the landless. *Bhoodan*, literally meaning 'gifting of land', was a step towards building an egalitarian rural society. As Bhave put it, 'The first step in the movement was that no person should be left landless in the village. The last is there should be no "land-owner" in the village. All land should belong to the Community' (Dhadda 2014). He also asked for *gramdan*, donation of an entire village voluntarily agreed by all the landholders. First ever *gramdan* took place in the village of Mangroth in Uttar Pradesh.

Bundelkhand and Chitrakoot

Chitrakoot District is located in the Bundelkhand region. A brief profile of the region is required to locate the context where the Kols live and the context of their struggle. Bundelkhand consists of seven districts in Uttar Pradesh and six in Madhya Pradesh. As per the 2011 census, a majority of people (79%) live in villages. The literacy rate is below the national and state average. Out of 13 districts in Bundelkhand, six districts in Uttar Pradesh and four in Madhya Pradesh were covered under the Backward Region Grant Fund. As cultivators and agricultural labourers, a majority of people are dependent on agriculture for their livelihood. Bundelkhand is inhabited by SC, ST, OBC and other general castes. Close to 25% of the population is SC, whereas the ST population constitutes a small percentage of the total population. However, there is a discrepancy between the two states regarding official recognition of tribal communities as ST. For example, the Kols are listed as a ST in Madhya Pradesh whereas they are listed as SC in Uttar Pradesh. Similarly, Shaharias are include as an ST only in Lalitpur District of Uttar Pradesh. The topography of Bundelkhand is characterized by hard rocks, poor soil quality, scant rainfall and water scarcity. These conditions make agriculture low yielding as well as risky. Bundelkhand is also drought-prone. It witnessed drought every

16 years during the 19th and 20th centuries. The frequency of droughts has increased in recent times. Failure of crop and credit has driven farmers to suicide. Food scarcity, hunger deaths and suicides are reported in the region. Chitrakoot District was earlier a part of Banda District; it was formed as a separate district in 1998. As per 2011 census, 90.29% of the district's population live in villages. Chitrakoot District was declared a drought-hit district in 2006.

The 1970s and the Foundation of ABSSS

The 1970s was a distinct period in Indian history, a period characterized by a trenchant critique of the state and growing dissent against it. After two decades of the optimism of nation-building, the discontents became visible. There were four major streams through which this discontent was articulated: The Naxalite Movement tried to address the land rights for the poor. It began in a small village of Naxalbari, Darjeeling, and quickly spread to other parts of West Bengal. It gathered a violent streak as the movement leaders began dispensing what they called justice. It built terror against the rich peasants as well as the state as the movement saw them working in alliance. The Sampoorn Kranti (Total Revolution) Movement spearheaded by Jayaprakash Narayan[2] organized students, workers, peasants, low castes and tribals. The movement articulated the growing inequality between the rich and the poor, and the need for the redistribution of resources. The 1970s was also a period when identity-based movements rose to articulate the interests of specific sections. The structural conditions of caste and patriarchy were articulated by Dalit and women movements respectively. The period witnessed the genesis of ecology movements that questioned the commercial use of natural resources on which poor people subsist. The first ever ecology movement was the Chipko Movement that opposed the commercial felling of

[2] Jayaprakash Narayan, popularly called JP, was a freedom fighter and socialist thinker.

trees in Uttarakhand. Subsequently, movements rose against commercial fishery, large dams, mining and power companies.

In this period, thick with discontent and dissent, ABSSS was founded in 1978 to address the grinding poverty, inequality and exploitation of the tribals and Dalits in Bundelkhand. It began its work among the Kol Tribals in Patha region, a further impoverished part of Bundelkhand, organizing them to assert their land rights and demand freedom from bonded labour. Founded on the Gandhian principles of non-violent struggle, rural reconstruction and *antodaya*[3] (rise of the last person), ABSSS has, in close to four decades, has addressed a gamut of issues, such as land rights, rehabilitation of bonded labour, access to natural resources such as forest and water, and access to government polices such as PDS, NREGA and drought relief.

Sangharsh (struggle) and *rachna* (construction/creation) have been the twin core principles guiding ABSSS. *Sangharsh* encompasses struggle to assert rights, dignity and equality, and *rachna* connotes the construction of a new society based on egalitarian principles as well as building a self-reliant economy.

After India gained independence, the Gandhian principles of rural reconstruction were adopted by the government to promote cottage industries and social upliftment through community development. ABSSS has infused the principles with a critical tinge by pursuing them in a rights-based framework. It has sought to engage with both the state and the wider society to weave a vision of social change that is founded on the principles of equality, dignity and social justice.

ABSSS began its work in a period when the state was merely responding to the views and actions emanating from the sphere of civil society; it had not yet constructed its own relationship, in its own terms, with any formally organized civil society such as ABSSS and other organizations that were founded during the 1970s and early 1980s. That happened much later when

[3] Gandhian philosophy and action that aim to bring the last person, the poorest of the poor, to the forefront of prosperity.

the state turned neoliberal and sought to bring CSOs into a collaborative mode for implementing its programmes. Civil society actors, prior to that, operated in the space where they strategized their relationship with the state.

ABSSS frames its action as 'critical engagement' with the state. It critiques the state for its failure to implement policies meant for the poor and socially disadvantaged; at the same time, it engages with the state in the implementation of those policies. It organizes people to protest even as it works with the government agencies and officials to implement the programmes. The two-way engagement through critique and collaboration is strategized as complementary, and not parallel, to each other in order to achieve the goal. Simultaneously, ABSSS organizes people to represent their cause. The non-violent struggle includes both resistance and assertion, and is directed at both the state and the larger social structures. People are also taken on the path of self-help and self-reliance to forsake their total dependency on the state and work towards improving their own situation even as they demand their rights and entitlements from the state. Reconstruction thus includes action that supports enhancement of the lives of the marginalized through the restructuring of economic, political and social relations. ABSSS's works cover a wide range, from land and forest rights to drought relief, food security and access to government-sponsored development programmes.

It may seem that the actors and interlocutors in civil society step in to fulfil the role of the state when the state in a democracy is absent in the lives of its marginalized populace. The state, however, is not completely absent. It is present in a myriad ways—in policies, in the bureaucracy in charge of those policies, in institutions responsible for implementation of the policies and in the alliances between the state and the powerful in society. Mapping the nature of the presence of the state reveals that the state intends to be a benevolent presence, while subverting its own intention in practice. In the microcosm of villages, where the land rights mobilization took place, this was evident in the form of the half-measured implementation of policies, in the form of collaboration with the landed upper caste, in the form of connivance to deprive the poor of government schemes and in the form of occasional presence of a few good officers, who want to make the policies work.

What ABSSS essentially does is to convert the most deprived people into citizens, that is, from being mere beneficiaries of the state patronage to active citizens who assert their rights. While the state grants rights and entitlements, these per se do not make people citizens as the fulfilment of these rights and entitlements still depends on the benevolence of the state. In situations where the state sabotages its own agenda of development, organizations such as ABSSS step in to mobilize people to act like citizens and demand for their rights. They, thus, turn the passive subjects to active citizens. In democratizing development, people act on two fronts—they democratize the state as well as the unequal social relations. Civil society, thus, performs the dual task of reforming the state as well as the wider society (Chandhoke 1995).

Kol Mobilization for Land Rights

The Kols were the inhabitants of forests from where they were gradually driven out as forests came under state control during the colonial period. The process of displacement continued after the Independence as the state increasingly brought forests under its management. The Kols were further displaced due to industrialization when dams, wildlife sanctuaries and factories encroached upon their land. The Ranipur Sanctuary, the Continental Glass Factory and the Uttar Pradesh Industrial Corporation acquired their land, displacing them from their habitat and livelihood (Joshi 2003; Singh 1993).

Kols, despite being tribal, are categorized as SC in Uttar Pradesh (whereas they are ST in the adjacent state of Madhya Pradesh). The categorization has implications for them because the developmental benefits in the forms of special grants, as also the special inalienable land rights that STs have that put restriction on transfer of tribal land to non-tribals, are not available to the Kols in Uttar Pradesh.

The region where ABSSS began its work is known as Patha, literally means rocky and barren, which is a severely impoverished part of Bundelkhand. Patha is characterized by entrenched socio-economic inequality. Brahmins and Thakurs, the two upper castes, are in possession of large landholdings and yield considerable social influence. Their connection with the local administration, particularly at the block and district, is well established (Joshi 2003). This had implications, as we will see in the following discussion, for the Kols securing land allotted to them under the land reforms. While the upper castes hold good quality land, the land belonging to Kols are often rocky, non-irrigable and thus remain barren or the yield is meagre. The landed upper castes are referred to as *dadu*, a pejorative term that connotes the power and influence they yield (Joshi 2003). *Dadus* have appropriated the land of the Kols through deceit and power, at times on 'gun points', by what is euphemistically referred to as 'muscle power' (Seabrook 1995, 39). *Dadus* had not only encroached and controlled land belonging to the Kols but had also kept the Kols in a state of continuous deprivation by keeping them under litigation and bondage.

Dadus controlled the land belonging to the Kols, as the Kols were not conversant with the legalities of land titles. As contractors with the forest department, *dadus* employed the Kols to cut woods and collect tendu leaves. The wages were paid in kind, that is, 1.25 kilograms of food grains for a day's labour (Singh 1993). This gave rise to indebtedness among the Kols. Taking advantage of the poverty and illiteracy among the Kols, *dadus* kept them under bondage; in many cases, an entire family worked as *beggar* (bonded labour) to *dadus*. The Kols often took debt from the upper castes both in cash and in food grain. They served as bonded labour until they paid off the debt. If they died, their children inherited the bondage. In some cases, the Kols were turned into bonded labours for small amounts of debt, and, in some cases, they remained in bondage for 20 long years (Joshi 2003). The bonded Kol women were often sexually exploited by their owners (Dogra 2000; Joshi 2003; Rashid 2013).

Dadus subverted the land ceiling act by transferring excess land to their Kol servants, who were unaware of this transfer and subsequent implications. It was only when they were harassed for the recovery of loans that the *dadus* had taken against their land, that they realized how they were further entrapped in bondage. Not only the landed households retained their land by taking advantage of their alliance with the administration and politicians, the ceiling surplus land allotted to the Kols were mere land titles, called *patta*, without actual possession. In many cases, the land allotted were of poor quality, rocky and non-irrigable; in some other cases, the allotted land came under dispute as the forest department claimed land to build a wild life sanctuary (Joshi 2003). *Dadus* encroached upon the good quality land allotted to the Kols through threat and/or deceit. There were instances where the land the Kols had taken on lease from the gram sabha and cultivated for 8–10 years were transferred to locally powerful people. In such cases, while the lease was recorded on revenue records of the panchayat, it was not marked on the map, thus creating a purposeful gap that was taken advantage of.[4]

It is in this situation that ABSSS intervened to mobilize the Kols in the Mau and Manikpur blocks of Chitrakoot District[5] to claim titles and possession of the land they were allotted under the land reforms. When ABSSS surveyed the villages, they found that the land reforms and land distribution were marred with fraud, widespread bondage and indebtedness among the Kols. The Kols thus lived in a state of landlessness, poverty and bondage.

Land distribution had received further impetus during the late 1970s and early 1980s to provide a pro-poor flavour to

[4] Personal communication with Bhagwat Prasad, the director of ABSSS, in 2016.
[5] The blocks were part of Banda District at that time.

governance in the aftermath of National Emergency. The National Emergency clamped by the ruling party to supress dissent was the darkest period in the history of democracy in the independent India; it had seen the suspension of the fundamental rights of people and the Constitution. There was also a latent objective in pushing pro-poor reforms during the period. It was to deter people from being radical in the wake of the Naxalite Movement in West Bengal where violent conflicts had taken place around land.

In 1987, ABSSS formed the Patha Kol Adhikar Manch[6] with membership from the Kols. The Manch has since then served as a platform for raising awareness among Kols and nurturing leadership among Kol youth. In the same year, ABSSS organized the Chitrakoot Patha Kol Vikas Vichar Gosthi[7] where the district collector of Banda announced that the Kols in Manikpur Block would soon get possession of the land allotted to them. A committee was constituted with 11 *lekhpals* (accountants), and 100 hectares of land was measured for distribution to the Kols. However, the effort stopped at that. There were pressures on the administration; it was believed that *dadus* had put pressure to close the process (Singh 1993).

ABSSS's work among the Kols included not only mobilizing to claim land promised under the land reforms but also freeing them from bondage and ensuring their rehabilitation. ABSSS's advocacy on bonded labour put pressure on the government, and then labour secretary initiated a study in the Manikpur and Shankargarh blocks of Chitrakoot District. The study found 2,900 bonded labour in Manikpur and 3,300 bonded labour in Shankargarh. Yet, the findings of the report could not force the government to take action (Singh 1993).

As a result of continuous advocacy on the issue by ABSSS, a bonded labour rehabilitation committee was constituted by the

[6] An organization of the Kols living in the Patha region to pursue their rights.

[7] Public discussion on the situation of the Kols in Patha region.

government. In 1983, a bonded labour rehabilitation office was created. The legalities prescribed that those who kept bonded labourer could just free them by giving them a few goats, buffalo and some cash (Singh 1993). No punishment was given to those who kept the Kols in bondage and practised bonded slavery. ABSSS stepped in to help the Kols get the rehabilitation grant.

In 1989, the chief minister of Uttar Pradesh revived the land distribution programme. The actual possession of land required two copies of the land deed with the signatures of the landholder and two witnesses. This measure was subverted by the local administration. Those who received the land deed on paper without actual possession of land said that the *lekhpal* got the paper signed by them not as a land deed but as census papers (Singh 1993). The illiteracy among the Kols was again taken advantage of.

Land distribution got a third lease of life in 1991. The prime minister, in an inter-chief ministerial meeting, asked the chief ministers of the states to complete the land allotment and possession by March 1992; 14 October 1992 was set as the last date for implementation of land reforms.

A study (Singh 1993) conducted in August 1993 in Manikpur and Mau revealed the following:

1. Around 1971, in Tokria village, 23 Kol persons were given 200 *bighas*[8] of ceiling surplus land. The land belonged to a member of legislative assembly of Banda. Although *patta* was given, the actual possession did not take place. The Kols were asked to take land other than the ceiling land allotted to them.
2. Land belonging to those not staying in the village was confiscated and their *pattas* were cancelled. In Mau tehsil, the Kols were settled in the Kalchiha colony by the government in 1974. In 1988, their *pattas* were cancelled and the land

[8] A measure of land area varying locally from 1/3 to 1 acre.

was put under village common without any information to the Kol families.

3. In Mangawan village, nine Kol persons were allotted 10 *bighas* of land. However, the actual possession did not take place.

4. In Chherihakhurd village, the land allotted to Kols was encroached upon by *dadus*.

5. In Nihi village, 135 Kol persons could not get the possession of land even though they were allotted the land *patta*. *Dadus* had encroached upon their land and pushed them out of the village.

6. In Gobarhai village, eight Kol persons were allotted land *pattas*, but the land was under the possession of the upper caste Brahmins.

The aforementioned illustrates the power nexus against which civil society has to struggle, and that this struggle is long and arduous. After years of mobilization by ABSSS and through their own organization, the Kols could not overtly challenge the local dominance. However, even though the results in terms of land possession and rehabilitation were limited, the mobilization was making the Kols aware of their bondage and dispossession. As Rajan Kol of Patha Kol Adhikar Manch said,

> Despite very adverse conditions, a growing number of Kol youths are coming forward to challenge this oppressive system, and change their life of exploitation and repression. The struggles of forest, land and water are moving ahead. The results can be seen in the improved living conditions of hundreds of families. (Dogra 2000, 5)

That the Kols could gather the courage to stop the district collector of Banda when he travelled in the Patha region on 2 September 1992 and seek an explanation from him on land reforms and the absence of development measures for the poor illustrates the rising awareness and collective strength among the Kols (Dogra 2000). This was an unprecedented act. Where did the hitherto voiceless get voice? How did people find the courage to ask questions to a state official? It was precisely at this moment that the subjects transcended the barrier to become citizens.

The actual possession of the ceiling land distributed to the Kols began to take place from 1995 onwards. By 1997, 2,500 Kol families in Mau and Manikpur were able to get possession of their land, a total 10,000 acres of land valued at 20 million rupees (Joshi 2003). By 2005, 5,000 Kol families got legal possession of their land, a total 15,000 acres.[9] The acceleration of the process took place when Mayawati, a Dalit leader, became the chief minister of Uttar Pradesh. With her coming to power, both administrative and political power shifted from the hands of the upper castes and the landed. It also gave the poor and the socially marginalized a sense of power. She directed the administration to expedite the cases of land possession. Several public hearing meetings took place in which the district magistrates and assistant district magistrates along with a large number of people participated.[10] The democratic decentralization that energized panchayats and local governance in the early 1990s was also instrumental in giving the Kols the possession of ceiling surplus land.[11]

Let me return to the questions I posed in the beginning: What value do people see in land ownership that inspires them to struggle hard to get possession of the land? What does the long struggle for a small patch of land mean to those who have been in bondage to the landed? A piece of land gets connotations when seen in the context of people who were displaced from their land, who were in bondage, and whose rights including land rights were curtailed. It does not end inequality; it does not make much impact on poverty; and it does not take them out of the poverty trap. What it does is to turn them from being landless into landowners, even if that is marginal; to turn them into farmers, even though they may continue to work as labour

---

[9] Personal communication with Bhagwat Prasad, the director of ABSSS, in 2016.

[10] Personal communication with Bhagwat Prasad, director of ABBBS, in 2016.

[11] Personal communication with Bhagwat Prasad, the director of ABBBS, in 2016.

to supplement their income. A piece of land brings dignity to people, who were hitherto considered slaves. It is also important to note that the battle was with those who had enslaved them, appropriated their land and deprived them from the benefits of land reforms.[12]

The following are some of the key strategies ABSSS used to mobilize the Kols. Since the organization continues working among the Kols, its subsequent work adds to the mobilization for land rights, thus turning the pursuit of development and social justice into a continuous process even after the larger goal for which the mobilization took place was achieved.

People's Organizations

People's organizations are the collectives through which mobilization takes place. During the land rights mobilization, ABSSS formed, facilitated and strengthened people's collectives to represent themselves. It built awareness and information, supported people in organizing rallies, dharnas (demonstration) and nurtured Kol leadership. The Patha Kol Adhikar Manch was formed to collectivize the Kols and build their own organization to address their cause. The Manch has membership from the Kols, which expanded over the years. ABSSS formed Mahila Samakhya groups as women collectives. Mahila Samakhya, a government programme, began in Chitrakoot around the same time as the Kol mobilization, and ABSSS took the lead to create Mahila Samakhya centres. During the four years, 1989–92, around 40 Mahila Samakhya centres were opened under the programme. The centres organized women collectives, gave information about their rights, encouraged women to send their daughters to school and encouraged women to speak against their exploitation. The centres not only created awareness among women but also helped women become leaders.

---

[12] Personal communication with the villagers who had received surplus ceiling land during my visit to Manikpur in 2008.

Forum for Public Discussion

ABSSS took the culture of public discussion to villages and organized Patha Kol Vichar Gosthi in villages to create awareness among the Kols. This provided Kol women a space to participate in the discussions. Kol women joined the struggle by forming women's groups. Women, who had hitherto worked as labourers, had remained in slavery, and had suffered sexual exploitation, organized themselves to speak up and confront their adversaries. On 12 March 1987, Kol women in Rampuria village stood against the sexual advancement made by the forest officials and went to the police station in Manikpur to lodge a complaint. Forest officials responded by implicating their husbands in illegal felling of trees in forests (Singh 1993). Women organized a rally and came together in large numbers to oppose this publicly. This gave courage to women in other villages to speak against the powerful, even against those who they were serving as bonded labour.

Public Space to Elicit Wider Support

One of the strategies of ABSSS is to bring the issues of poverty and exploitation into public discussion. It creates public space for people who otherwise remain invisible. Through public hearings, seminar and discussions, it creates an interface between the people and the government on the one hand, and between people and opinion makers, such as academics and journalists, on the other. The public discussion platforms are also shared by people such as government officials, lawyers and jurists, academics and media whose support is essential to ABSSS work. Public discussions also serve as spaces for awareness building among people who are at the helm of the struggle and create a wider social environment in which those struggles are waged.

During the land rights mobilization, ABSSS organized Patha Kol Adhikar Vichar Gosthi and Kol women's public hearing. On 19 May 1997, a public hearing was organized by ABSSS to encourage Kol women speak publicly about their exploitation.

The meeting was attended by Mohini Giri, the then chairperson of the National Commission for Women. Three hundred Kol women presented their case publicly. She later wrote to Mayawati, the then chief minister of Uttar Pradesh. A committee was organized to study the conditions of Kol women and report to government. She also helped organizing a similar public hearing in Delhi as well. This brought the issues to limelight, encouraged women to speak and gave them visibility.

Subsequently, as it began addressing drought, poverty and hunger deaths, it organized a public hearing in Chitrakoot. Close to eight hundred people from different districts of Bundelkhand participated in the hearing which was attended by eminent jurists, government representatives, academics and journalists.

Legal Aid

Legal aid remains an important aspect of ABSSS's work. During the land rights mobilization, the organization held legal aid camps for people whose land rights were violated through deceitful means. ABSSS supported the Kols in identifying the cases, drafting legal application and engaging lawyers to fight the cases. By focussing on legal aspects of rights as a core part of social mobilization, ABSSS built the capacity of the poor and the socially marginalized to interface with law and agencies such as police and courts. Its legal support centre not only supports people in dealing with the legal aspects of their rights but also takes recourse to legal action for implementation of the rights through public interest litigation. A large number of legal cases in which the organization has helped people are related to land. However, there are also cases seeking entitlements under various state-sponsored development schemes.

Self-Reliance

At the same time, as it was mobilizing the Kols for their land rights, the organization was also working towards creating a self-reliant economy for the Kols. ABSSS's work was not confined to mobilizing the Kols to assert their land rights and getting the land title and actual possession of land but also supported them in cultivating the land once they got possession. Once land was transferred to the titleholder, the next step was to improve land quality and augment water resources to make the land cultivable. In a majority of cases, the land given to the Kols was not of good quality, and the holdings were small in size. Hence, to eke out a living, the land had to be improved to be cultivable and the yield had to be good. ABSSS supported people in reviving the traditional structures of rainwater harvesting such as wells, small ponds and check dams. The work had begun in 1982, and the reservoirs had proved beneficial. This generated eagerness among people and the organization has continued the water conservation work.[13]

The land rights struggle of the Kols shows that social justice in some situations is a precondition for the economic development of the most marginalized people. For people who were in bondage, a minimum-level playing field was required for them to claim their land rights. This case shows why civil society intervention is essential to democratize development, and also the limits of democratization. Neither the state is reformed once and for all nor are the social powers contained once and for all. Democratization is a continuous process civil society actors have to engage with. Therefore, building people's organization and empowering them are critical to sustain the struggle, and making people self-reliant is as essential as mobilizing them for their rights.

[13] During 2008–09, ABSSS started a water project in five villages—Mangawan, Bambia, Tikaria, Jamunihai and Doda Mafi—to augment water resources and improve agriculture and livelihood. Sajal Committees were formed as community organization to work on the project. Gradually, people began to build water conservation structures such as farm ponds, ponds and check dams. Despite low rainfall, almost 61 farm ponds and ponds could hold sufficient rainwater, and the wells had water even during peak summers. Within a span of three years, agricultural yields increased for the Kol farmers (CSE 2012).

References

Akhil Bhartiya Samaj Seva Sansthan (ABSSS). n.d. *Rachna Evam Sangharsh ke Do Dashak*. Chitrakoot: ABSSS.

Besley, T., and Burgess, R. 2000. 'Land Reforms, Poverty Reduction, and Growth: Evidence from India'. *Quarterly Journal of Economics* 115 (2): 389–430.

Chandhoke, N. 1995. *Civil Society and the State*. New Delhi: SAGE.

Centre for Science and Environment (CSE). 2012. *Water Wise: The Journey from Bonded Labour to Water Warriors*. Available at http://www.cse.org.in/content/water-wise-journey-bonded-labourers-water-warriors

Dhadda, S. 2014. 'Vinoba Bhave's Gramdan Movement'. Satyagraha Foundation. Available at http://www.satyagrahafoundation. org/vinoba-bhaves-gramdan-movement/

Dogra, B. 2000. *Fighting Terror, Protecting Dignity: ABSSS Gives Kol Tribals New Hope. Report on a Voluntary Organizations Work in Chitrakoot Region*. Self-published booklet, New Delhi.

Food First Information and Action Network (FIAN). 2004. *International Fact Finding Mission: Investigating Violation of the Right to Food in Uttar Pradesh*. Norway: FIAN.

Joshi, B. K. 2003. 'Distribution of Land Patta to Kol Tribals'. In *Does Civil Society Matter? Governance in Contemporary India*, edited by R. Tandon and R. Mohanty. New Delhi: SAGE.

Rashid, O. 2013. 'Kols in Chitrakoot: A Life Without Rights'. *The Hindu*, 10 April.

Seabrook, J. 1995. *Notes from Another India*. London: Pluto Press.

Singh, H. P. 1993. *Dharti ka Dard*. Chitrakoot: ABSSS.

Vachhani, A., Tripathy, S., and Singh, V. 2009. *Ceiling Land Distribution in Uttar Pradesh: Implications on the Marginalized Sections*. Mussoorie: LBS National Academy of Administration.

7

Collective Economies of the Poor
The Ethics of Equity

Capitalist economies, with the added impetus from globalization, deprive the poor of their livelihood resources by divert-
ing them for commercial use, impoverishing them further
by excluding them from the benefits of growth and pushing
them out from the formal economy into the precarious and
unprotected realm of the informal economy. In the face of this
ruthlessness and marginalization, the poor create their own
economies by pooling in their resources. In doing this, the poor
not only create economies that are different from the dominant
economy in their modes of organization, production and distribution, but the collective economies are also an indication of
the possibilities of other economies. Called variously as community economy, solidarity economy and alternative economy,
the collective economies are essentially what Gibson-Graham
(2006) calls 'post capitalist' that are heralding a different economic model that has emerged in response to the fallouts of
the dominant model of development. In this sense, the collective economies are also post-development economies (Escobar
1995). Based on the principles of 'reciprocity and redistribution'

(McNally 2006), these alternative economies defy profit-oriented exclusionary economies of growth and globalization. The collective economies present a diverse range—from grain banks that tribal people have created in southern Odisha to deal with food scarcity to autonomous self-regulated economic zones that Zapatista Movement has created for the indigenous people in Chiapas in Mexico, from people in Rajasthan who are reviving their traditional water harvesting system to augment water resources to an alternative currency system in Spain. Their local contexts are different, but what is common to them is that in the face of a ruthless capitalist order, people are creating their own economic systems through their collective agency.

This chapter discusses the collective economies the poor in India have been creating for their subsistence. Of the diverse types of collective economies that are being pursued by the poor, the economies based on the ecological resources of land, water and forests are discussed to elaborate how the *economic nomads* of the growth economy are creating alternative *ecological economies*. These economies function on the basis of collective resources, collective ownership and collective management. The distributive principles of these collective economies are based on the ethics of equity. The chapter presents three examples of collective economies briefly, and subsequently analyses their functioning and their potential for the democratic use of ecological resources as well as the democratic distribution of benefits.

Collective Economies in India

Collective economies of the poor are not new in India. They have coexisted along with the dominant economy of growth as surviving mechanisms to cope with the onslaught of growth. The collective economies are different in their membership, objectives and modes of operation.

One of the most widely known examples of collective economy is Self Employed Women's Association (SEWA), a trade union of informal women workers. Started in 1972 with women working as casual labourers in the textile markets of Ahmedabad, SEWA's membership has grown into thousands over the years. SEWA members are both rural and urban poor who work in the informal economies, and therefore, remain unprotected. SEWA works as both a trade union and a collective of women entrepreneurs. While the trade union works for securing workers' rights such as employment security, income security, food security and social security, the SEWA cooperatives organize and market their commodities such as dairy and crafts.

The state has an enormous presence in collective economies as it promotes such economies as a strategy for poverty eradication. The state-sponsored programmes on poverty reduction have a natural resource management component that aims at sustainable use and management of common resources on which village people are dependent for their livelihood. The watershed management projects improve soil quality, construct irrigation structures and promote afforestation. The forest management projects promote social forestry and protect the reserved forests. The projects constitute users group or community institutions for the sharing of benefits and maintenance of assets created by the projects. That, however, does not guarantee community involvement in the management of resources or their sustainable use primarily because of state control. The assets created are handed over to the panchayats for maintenance, and it then becomes the responsibility of panchayats to manage the resources after the project period is over. In those cases where panchayats engage people, community involvement does take place.

Collectives of women farmers are formed by both the state and civil society initiatives. The women collectives are constituted mostly by landless women and marginal women farmers, a majority of who work as casual agriculture labour. The women farmers take wasteland or fallow land on lease. The collectives primarily work to ensure food security for the members as well as a source of income generation. The women famers' collectives are being constituted in a context when agriculture is given a low priority in economic growth policies, and agricultural land, water and forest resources are diverted for industrial growth. The rural poor dependent on agriculture are threatened with food scarcity, hunger and migration. Globalization has intensified the process as multinational companies claim the resources of the poor. For instance, Coca Cola extracts water resources; Vedanta mining displaces people from their land, habitat and livelihood.

Cooperatives are trade-related collectives formed to support the members in a variety of ways such as production, protection, marketing and provision for credit. Among a diverse range of cooperatives, the prominent ones are those constituted by farmers, weavers, crafts persons, dairy producers and fishermen. Cooperatives are regulated by the state laws. Cooperatives started in India during the colonial period when farmers cooperatives were formed for credit purpose. After independence, cooperatives were mainstreamed into development planning as vehicles for poverty eradication. One of the best known cooperatives is Amul, the milk producers' cooperative that has grown in size and business. The cooperative movement in India has suffered due to state interference, excess dependence on the state and compromise on the basic principles of self-reliance and equity.

Microfinance groups of women, popularly known as SHG, are a ubiquitous presence in Indian villages. Formed under various poverty eradication programmes, including the most recent Aajeevika,[1] SHGs represent microfinance as a vehicle for the economic development of the rural people. SHGs work as saving and credit groups, and they are linked to banks to facilitate their access to credit. SHGs are promoted as women's collectives to work as entrepreneurs and engage its members in income generation by pursuing economic activities collectively. Even though microfinance is promoted on such a large scale, not all SHGs demonstrate the capacity to function as entrepreneurs—many

[1] NRLM is called Aajeevika (livelihood).

groups become dormant as they cannot pay back the loan taken from the bank, and many continue only as mechanisms for inter-loaning to group members in times of need. CSOs often work with SHGs and promote them as community organizations for their programmes that range from livelihood, health and education to women empowerment.

Three Cases of Successful Collective Economies

Sangha Krishi

Sangha Krishi, literally meaning group farming, is practised by the landless women in Kerala villages. The women lease wasteland and fallow land, improve the soil quality and cultivate a variety of crops and vegetables. There are around 46,000 of such women's collectives engaged in farming (Sainath and Mukherjee 2015). Dalits, tribals and minorities constitute close to half of the membership in these collectives (Mukherjee 2012). The yield from the land is either sold in the market or taken home when there is a shortage of food for family members. In the village of Perambra, women have leased 140 acres of fallow land that had remained uncultivated for 26 years and have converted it into cultivable land (Sainath and Mukherjee 2015).

Sangha Krishi was initiated in 2007 under the poverty eradication programme of the government of Kerala. The women collectives called Kudumbashree (family prosperity) began in 1998 under the 'People's Plan' which envisaged the inclusion of marginalized women at the grassroots in decentralized local governance with an aim to provide them a space for association outside their homes and inclusion of their voice in local planning and development. Subsequently, Kudumbashree collectives have become an active part of the decentralized governance. Simultaneously, they are engaged in multiple income-generation enterprises. Kudumbashree women have been able to build a solidarity network of close to four million women (Mukherjee-Reed 2015).

As Kudumbashree members, the women farmers pursuing Sangha Krishi are part of the three tier structure that comprises a Neighbourhood Group which has 10–20 poor women members at the village level, an Area Development Society which is a federation of NHGs at the ward level, and a Community Development Society which is again a federation of ADSs at the panchayat level. As parts of a state-led programme, Sangha Krishi and Kudumbashree are facilitated, regulated and monitored by the state agencies.

Collective economies such as Sangha Krishi are significant for the rural poor, and have an impact on their lives in ways that are critical not only for their economic well-being but also for their dignity, rights and justice. Despite having a PDS for food, the rural poor suffer from hunger, food scarcity and malnutrition. In such situations, an initiative such as Sangha Krishi provides food security to a family as well as to a community. At another level, it turns landless women, majority of who work as agriculture labour, into farmers. As a result of Sangha Krishi, as Mukherjee (2012) puts it,

> There is a palpable shift in the role of women in Kerala's agriculture. This was earlier limited to daily wage work in plantations, at wages much lower than those earned by men. Thousands of Kudumbashree women—hitherto underpaid agricultural labourers—have abandoned wage work to become independent producers. Many others combine wage work with farming. With independent production comes control over one's time and labour, over crops and production methods and, most significantly, over the produce. Since the farmers are primarily poor women, they often decide to use a part of their produce to meet their own needs, rather than selling it. Every group takes this decision democratically, depending on levels of food insecurity of their members. In Idukki, where the terrain prevents easy market access and food insecurity is higher, farmers take more of their produce home as opposed to Thiruvananthapuram where market access is better and returns are higher.

At a time when agriculture is neglected by the policymakers forcing farmers to opt out of agriculture, Sangha Krishi restores agriculture as a viable livelihood option. At a time when large swaths of agricultural land is given to industries and corporations, poor women, working collectively, have been reviving wastelands, thus turning them productive. Even though the landless women don't become landowners, in an economic and social setting where poor women struggle to earn livelihood, Sangha Krishi has provided them dignity of livelihood, and seek what Mukherjee (2012) calls 'food justice'.

Grain Bank

Grain bank, locally called *kutumb panthy* (community fund) is a collective storage build through contribution of grain by the members for the purpose of consumption in the lean period when food is short in supply or not available. The tribal communities in the southern Odisha villages have built grain banks as a measure against poverty, food scarcity, hunger and malnutrition. Each household contributes to the bank rice and millet that they cultivate, and each is given a share, in the form of a loan, from the bank depending on their need. The members pay an interest fee on the loan. They pay off the loan as well as the fee during harvest, and that keeps the stock replenished.

Agragamee, a grassroots organization working among the tribal communities in southern Odisha initiated grain bank in 1983, and since then the grain banks have increased in number. The tribal communities at that time were facing immense deprivation and hardship—landlessness, meagre income from working as wage labour, unemployment due to seasonal nature of work, lack of financial resources to invest in agriculture, dependency on monsoon for agriculture, crop failure, indebtedness, food scarcity and malnutrition. Food scarcity was so severe that people were forced to eat mango kernels that they soaked and dried (Reddy and Adolf 2002).

Each grain bank started with an initial food grain contribution from members and a matching amount from Agragamee. Agragamee also trained the villagers in grain bank management. Each grain bank is managed by a village committee that oversees the collection, distribution, account keeping and storage. The decision to distribute food grain as per household needs is decided by the village. Even though an interest fee is charged, it is relaxed for households that cannot pay the interest. They are given a longer time to settle the interest. The grain bank and the villagers ensure that no one remains hungry in the village for lack of food (WFP 2006).

The grain banks, besides providing food security to people, have saved them from money lenders and rescued them from the trap of indebtedness. The collective efforts of people have motivated them to cultivate *donger* (hill) land as also land that had remained uncultivated due to lack of seed and fertilizer (WFP 2006). In some villages, women have started separate grain banks as well as grain banks for children (WFP 2006). As in the case of Sangha Krishi, grain banks have provided the tribal communities food justice and dignity in livelihood. The success of grain banks has resulted in Odisha Household Food Security Project, a state-funded project in select tribal districts (Giri 2005).

Following the success of grain banks, Agragamee has initiated grain-cum-seed banks. People store seeds such as beans, tomato, cowpea, *kandul* (pigeon pea) and pumpkin in the bank (Agragamee 2016). The seed banks perform two important functions: They preserve the genetic diversity of seeds that are destroyed by climate change and the use of chemically harmful fertilizers and pesticides, and build stock and provide the farmers seed during seed loss or shortage that occur due to the late arrival of monsoon or flash flood (Mohanty and Sahu 2016). The seed banks use the indigenous knowledge women have in seed preservation.

Johad

Johad is a traditional rainwater harvesting practise in Rajasthan. Rajasthan being the driest state in the country has limited surface water. Agriculture and livestock constitute sources of livelihoods for the rural population. Agriculture in Rajasthan is rain-fed. Ground water is the main source for irrigation, drinking, and other domestic use.

Johads are a system of earthen check dams that arrest runoff leading to improvement in percolation and groundwater recharge. The water collected in a *johad* during the monsoon is used for irrigation, drinking and other domestic purposes. *Johads* improve the soil moisture in the fields, and, as a result, during winter, it can help in cultivating a second crop.

Although *johads* are a traditional system to check rainwater runoff and recharge ground water, the practice was neglected due to extracting technology of ground water to meet the needs of a growing population and livestock, state intervention in water management and increasing dependency on the state leading to loss of local knowledge, loss of local technology and disintegration of community organizations (Singh n.d.).

Tarun Bharat Sangh (TBS), a grassroots organization based in Thanagazi Block in Alwar District, began reviving *johads* with community support. It began its work in Gopalpura village in 1985, and, in 25 years, it has built close to 10,000 water structures in 1,000 villages spread over 15 districts in Rajasthan (Sisodia 2009). *Johads* are constructed on both the agricultural land and the village common land (*gochar*). They are constructed by using local knowledge, local resources and locally available technology. Modern technology is used in a limited manner, and only when it is required.

TBS works on the principles of community-based water management through local organizations that it has helped constitute. Jal Samiti (water committee) and Jal Sabha (water assembly) are two such collectives that help in planning, construction and maintenance of *johads*. As representative of village residents, the community organizations are also responsible for including the land belonging to all social groups while planning *johads*. All decisions regarding *johads* are taken by gram sabha.

People who would benefit from a *johad* share 30% of the cost of construction.[2]

Johads ensure both conservation and prudent use of natural resources, and help restore ecological balance and biodiversity. The *johads* constructed by TBS have resulted in an increase in ground water level; they have resulted in sustained increase in crops, increase in household income from agriculture and animal husbandry, and have stopped migration to other regions for work (Sinha et al. 2013).

The aforementioned three cases indicate the following:

1. Collective economies are means for subsistence for the poor who live on the periphery and, in some instances, outside the market economy. Excluded by the growth economy, they organize to create their own economies. As they grow, they even try to enter the market economy although that entry can only be marginal.
2. Collective resource is the key resource that the poor harness to organize in a collective economy. The CBOs not only provide collective strength that the poor need, they also ensure that collective economies are made egalitarian. Collective subsistence, not individual profit, remains the key purpose of collective economies of the poor.
3. Collective economies revive local indigenous knowledge and traditional wisdom including traditional technologies. This partly comes from the lack of resources to avail modern technologies. The poor, however, access modern technologies if they consider it useful. For example, while TBS constructs *johads* using traditional knowledge and technologies, it consults engineers when required. Collective economies do not discard modern information, knowledge and technologies altogether; they use them selectively.
4. Collective economies practice equity not in a rationally calculated 'equal share for equal contribution' way; rather,

---

[2] Personal communication with Chaman Singh, TBS, in 2016.

equity in collective economies is need-based allocation of resources and benefits. Equity in collective economies encompasses the values of empathy and compassion. As the practice of grain banks shows, even when a household is not able to contribute to the grain bank or has exhausted the amount to be given as a loan or lacks the resources to pay off the loan and fee during next harvest, the household still gets grain from the bank. Such households are given an extended period to return the amount of grain they owe to the grain bank.

5. Collective economies conserve, respect and make prudent use of natural resources. As the economies are based on need, as opposed to the greed of the growth economy, people care and harness the resources. As the survival of the poor depends on the ecological resources of land, water and forest, collective economies have positive impact on ecology as they strive towards sustainability and biodiversity.

6. Collective economies save the poor from food scarcity, hunger, malnutrition, indebtedness and migration. In doing so, they not only bestow dignity on the most deprived population but also make them articulate and seek distributive justice that encompasses access to resources, livelihood and food. Resonating the social movements that are articulating rights that are not enshrined in the Constitution but are emanating from the loss of resources and livelihoods, the collective economies are articulating justice that are not legal but are emanating from their battle to have locally based livelihoods.

Economy, Ecology and Equity

Localism and Globalism

Collective economies are to be viewed as both local and global. The economies are locally anchored, that is, the action is at the local level, where the poor live and pursue their livelihood. The global forces that affect the local economies, for example, genetically modified seeds that deprive the farmers of indigenous seeds or mining that displaces people from their livelihood and habitat, are countered through global alliances with similarly positioned actions.

Local economies are a response to counter the global capitalist economy. Local economies are not only local spaces where they are pursued but also are economies that represent the construction of economies in non-capitalist ways. In this spanning of local to global, the emphasis, however, remains on the local. The local provides a context to collective economies, and the local is also a way of escaping from the fierceness of the global as people escape the 'globalization of their marginality by turning to localization' (Esteva and Prakash 1997, 282).

The economies resonate with Gandhi's idea of the village republic and its mode of production. As Gandhi envisaged,

> My idea of Village Swaraj is that it is a complete republic, independent of its neighbours for its own vital wants, and yet interdependent for many others in which dependence is a necessity. Thus, every village's first concern will be to grow its own food crops and cotton for its cloth. It should have a reserve for its cattle... if there is more land available, it will grow useful money crops.... (1962, 44)

> ... the economic constitution of India and for the matter of that of the world should be such that no one under it should suffer from want of food and clothing. In other words everybody should be able to get sufficient work to enable him to make the two ends meet. And this ideal can be universally realized only if the means of production of the elementary necessaries of life remain in the control of the masses. (1962, 46)

Ecological Economies and Equity

Collective economies are created by people who are the worst sufferers of ecological loss and degradation—people who the loss turns into economic nomads. The ecological and economic loss takes place in three prominent ways:

1. Industrial expansion displaces people from their livelihood and habitat (Chapter 2 discusses this in details).
Development conceived as public good allows the state to
take the land, water and forests on which people have been
subsisting for generations.
2. Degradation of natural resources due to over use, breakdown
of traditional management systems, state control on natural
resources and dependency on the state lead to loss of local
resources.
3. The changed pattern of agriculture involving biotechnology,[3]
high cost and low output, over utilization of fertilizers and
pesticides leading to soil degradation, inadequate markets
and markets geared for export and import and indebtedness
among farmers push them out from villages. As large part
of agriculture in India is rain-fed, the situation gets further
aggravated due to drought. It is small farmers who bear the
brunt.

Pushed out from their villages, lands and from their economies,
people who exist on the periphery of the market economy try
to enter it. But they can only enter it as casual wage workers,
domestic workers, slum dwellers and the urban poor. Collective
economies save them from this indignity. The loss of ecological
resources caused by the growth economy, as Sachs (1997, 296)
says, 'threats life-support systems in two ways: that of people
immediately and that of the biosphere in the long run. The
crisis of nature and the crisis of justice coincide for large part of
the world population in the experience of being marginalized
by "expansionist development"'.

[3] Vandana Shiva (2016), a leading advocate against Monsanto's
genetically modified Bt cotton is of the view that the genetically modified seeds have deprived the cotton growers in India of their traditional
seed. These seeds have increased the price of seeds, exponentially
leading indebtedness among farmers. Besides, the Bt cotton touted as
pest-resilient, in fact, is attacked by whitefly epidemic. She links the
farmers suicides in the cotton belts to these seeds.

The fate of people whose economies are built on natural resources thus hinges on protecting, reviving and using the resources in a sustainable manner. Collective economies based on ecological resources rescue people from loss of livelihoods and protect their resource base. They help address both the concerns that Sachs (1997) has pointed out—the crisis of nature and the crisis of justice.

Collective economies based on ecological resources are the opposite of growth economy in their philosophical foundation, modes of organization, objectives and values. Collective ecological economies are structurally oriented towards collective ownership, management and decision-making. The resources are not extracted for profit, but for the sustenance of people who depend on the resources for livelihood. As subsistence economies, equity is integral to collective economies. Equity does not only imply equal distribution of what people produce collectively but also need-based distribution ensuring that each member gets a share irrespective of actual contribution of resources. Hence, if the poor are building a grain bank economy, they ensure that no member household remains hungry because they could not contribute their share to the bank or they have already exhausted their quantity of loan from the bank. If women come together to cultivate farms, they work on the principle that a household takes the produce home when there is a need, and the surplus goes to the market. The ethics of equity and the distributive justice are built on the values of care and compassion.

Pachgaon, a predominantly tribal village in the Gondpipri Taluka of the Chandrapur District of Maharashtra, shows how people can manage forest resources prudently and plan livelihoods which care for ecology and equity (Gutgutia et al. 2017). Only a few households of Pachgaon practise cultivation; remaining households are heavily dependent on wage labour. As earning livelihoods became increasingly difficult, people faced the inevitable fate of migration. It was in this situation that the gram sabha of Pachgaon pursued getting Community Forest Rights (CFRs) under the Forest Right Act,

2006, although it was not an easy task and entailed many trips to the offices at the district, which people funded through their own contribution. The village was granted a total forest area of 2,486.90 acre for community management. Pachgaon people demarcated 85 acre as *devrai* (sacred grove). They have evolved a community plan to manage and use the forests sustainably for a variety of purposes such as bamboo harvest, fuel, fodder and livestock grazing.

Pachgaon people cultivate bamboo as a livelihood pursuit. The forest area is divided into three zones, and bamboo is cut in each zone once in three years. Bamboo is cut during November–May, and the plantation is left to grow during the rainy months from July to October. Sufficient time is thus given for the forest to regenerate. Cutting bamboo itself generates employment for the villagers. The wages are paid out of the sale of bamboo. The gram sabha auctions bamboo after deciding the rate. The surplus after the wages are paid is distributed among the villagers. People deposit 10% of their wages with the gram sabha, and they take their share during the four rainy months when they have no other employment.

All decisions regarding the management and use of forest is taken by the gram sabha. The gram sabha elects representatives from among the villagers to oversee the management of forest. The gram sabha holds at least four–five meetings every month, and the meetings are mandatory for the villagers. Each meeting is presided over by a village resident, and male and female residents rotate as the presidents of the meetings.

The gram sabha has laid out rules for the management and use of community forest: Every visitor to the forest has to sign a register and explain the purpose; villagers are assigned the responsibility of guarding the forests, and they do it in a group of five; fines are levied for stealing wood from the forest; grazing in the forest is allowed only between June–April, and two persons from the village take the cattle and goats from the village for grazing in the forest; grazing is not allowed in the sacred grove and in the bamboo cutting zone; and any conflict regarding the use of forest with the neighbouring villages is resolved in the gram sabha.

Threats to Collective Economies

Collective economies face the threat from commercial interests including the state's commercial projects. While the state organizes collective economies under various poverty eradication programmes, it also encroaches upon people's common resources and destroy their economy when its economic growth interests require the resources. An example of fishery in Chilika Lake will illustrate this clash of interest (Mohanty 2003).

The traditional fishing communities claim their fishing rights up to the British period. In order to protect the interest of fishermen and eliminate the non-fishermen and traders encroaching on the rights of the fishermen, the first cooperative society, Balugaon Fishermen Cooperative Store, was established in 1926 at Balugaon, Puri. It brought 24 fisheries under it. After the abolition of the estates and with the fishery sources coming within the preview of the government of Odisha in 1953, they were leased out by the government through open auction to the fishermen. The non-fishermen were allowed to take a limited number of fisheries. This practice continued until 1959 when the Central Cooperative Marketing Society was established in Balugaon. The Central Society was designed to act as an apex body that would take lease from the government and sublease them to the primary fishermen cooperatives. Most of the important fishery sources were subleased to the primary societies. In case there was no primary society, fisheries were subleased to villages dominated by fishermen. Those sources which were not taken on lease by the Central Society were auctioned. The Chilika Reorganisation Scheme thus made a clear-cut distinction between fishermen and non-fishermen and gave non-fishermen limited right to the lake.

The Government of Odisha issued an order in 1991 that divided the fisheries in Chilika into two categories—capture and culture. Capture rights were confined to the fishermen, and culture was opened to the non-fishermen and those villages which were not members of primary societies. Since culture fishery is more lucrative, the lake has been witnessing widespread subletting of leased out fisheries and illegal encroachment by both local non-fishermen and outsiders. This culturing of prawn on a big scale has resulted in the widespread conversion of traditional fisheries into prawn culture ponds or net enclosed *gheries* (barricaded space). Culture fishery requires heavy capital investment but ensures big profit. Hence, many primary societies have found it a lucrative source of income to lease it out to resourceful persons.

This widespread culturing of prawn has threatened the livelihood of traditional fishermen as well as the ecosystem of the lake. Thousands of fishermen and non-fishermen families have lost their livelihood due to conversion of traditional fishing sources into culture fishery. Cases of litigation and *prawn politics* now define the lives of the people in Chilika. Besides large-scale obstruction and blockade in the water channels, it obstructs the free flow of water, free migration of fish juveniles and loss of grazing ground for the fish. The *gheries* also act as silt traps and accelerate the process of siltation. The Integrated Shrimp Farm Project (ISFP), a joint semi-intensive prawn culture project between the Government of Odisha and the business house of the Tata, was given an advance possession of 400 hectares of land in Chilika, which was withdrawn following protest by fishermen. The encroachment on the fishery resources of the lake by the rich and influential, however, continues.

Role of the State

The state by virtue of being the prime actor of development plays an important role in collective economies. As cases discussed in this chapter show, the state can do both, facilitate collective economies or obstruct them. Where the commercial interests of the state overrides the livelihoods of poor, it encroaches upon their resources. In other situations, when it is not encroaching on people's livelihood resources, the state assumes the role of owner, controller and manager of resources. This not only alienates people but also creates dependency on the state, whereas when people are given ownership and left to manage the resources, they do so in a prudent manner. For instance, JFM, discussed earlier, despite being based on a model of partnership between the state and people, could not engage participation beyond employment in the project. The project, except for a few castes, gave rise to conflict of interests between the state and local communities as well as conflicts between various groups within a village community. In contrast, in Pachgaon, where the village has CFRs, people collectively manage the forest in such a manner that while the forest becomes a source of livelihood, it is also protected and used sustainably. As Guha and Gadgil (1995, 146) put it aptly,

> on all criteria—motivation, knowledge, management capabilities—the local communities are the most appropriate agency to look after and organize fine-tuned prudent use of India's natural resources base, whether of forests, grazing grounds, irrigation tanks, or agricultural lands. The state and the technically more sophisticated people, of course, have an important role to play, but that role should be of facilitation, coordination, of adding information not available to the local communities. Instead the state and its technocracy have assumed a very different role: that of agent of an extractive economy with no interest in prudent, sustainable resource use, controlling resource base, claiming monopoly over all pertinent information and making all decisions on how to deal with the natural resources of the country.

Collective economies are subsistence economies of the poor that cater to their bare survival. In the face of exclusion from the capitalist market economies, people come together to build self-reliant economies that at once help them survive the onslaught of the market and defy the capitalist logic of extraction and appropriation of resources. They bestow the vulnerable lone individual of the capitalist system with collective agency and solidarity of network. People do not shun the market altogether, instead they gather the resources to deal with the market economy and even try to make profit. Essential from the perspective of collective economies is principles of collective ownership and ethics of equity in distribution of benefits based on local knowledge and sustainable use of resources.

References

Agragamee. 2016. *Annual Report 2015–2016.* Kashipur: Agragamee. Available at http://agragamee.org/wp-content/uploads/2017/02/Annual-Report-2015-16.pdf

Escobar, A. 1995. *Encountering Development: The Making and Unmaking of the Third World.* Princeton, NJ: Princeton University Press.

Esteva, G., and Prakash, M. S. 1997. 'From Global Thinking to Local Thinking'. In *The Post-development Reader,* edited by M. Rehnama and B. Victoria. London: Zed Books.

Gandhi, M. K. 1962. *Village Swarajya.* Compiled by H. M. Vyas. Ahmedabad: Navajivan Publishing House.

Gibson-Graham, J. K. 2006. *A Postcapitalist Politics.* Minneapolis, MN: University of Minnesota Press.

Giri, A. 2005. *Reflections and Mobilization: Dialogue with Movements and Voluntary Organizations.* New Delhi: SAGE.

Guha, R., and Gadgil, M. 1995. *Ecology and Economy: The Use and Abuse of Nature in Contemporary India.* New Delhi: Penguin.

Gutgutia, S., Chowdhary, K., and Patil, R. 2017. 'Forest Conservation and Management in Pachgaon'. 20 June. Available at http://www.vikalpsangam.org/article/forest-conservation-and-management-in-pachgaon/

McNally, D. 2006. *Another World is Possible: Globalization & Anti-capitalism.* Winnipeg: Arbeiter Ring Publishing.

Mohanty, A., and Sahu, R. K. 2016. 'Seed Banks in the Centre of Origin: The Fight Against Climate Change'. *Jharkahnd Journal of Development and Management Studies* 14 (2): 6971–86.

Mohanty, R. 2003. 'Save the Chilika Movement: Civil Society Interrogating the State and the Market'. In *Does Civil Society Matter? Governance in Contemporary India,* edited by R. Mohanty and R. Tandon. New Delhi: SAGE.

Mukherjee, A. 2012. 'From Food Security to Food Justice'. *The Hindu*, 1 February.

Mukherjee-Reed, A. 2015. 'Taking Solidarity Seriously: Analyzing Kerala's Kudumbashree as Women's SSE Experience'. In *Social and Solidarity Economy: Beyond the Fringe*, edited by P. Utting. London: Zed Books.

Sachs, W. 1997. 'The Need for Home Perspective'. In *The Post-development Reader*, edited by M. Rehnama and V. Bawtree. London: Zed Books.

Sainath, P., and Mukherjee, A. 2015. 'Rural Women: Milestones, Millstones and Millionaires'. *People's Archive of Rural India*, 15 January. Available at https://ruralindiaonline.org/articles/rural-women-milestones-millstones-millionaires

Shiva, V. 2016. *Monsanto vs. Indian Farmers*. Available at http://vandanashiva.com/

Singh, R. n.d. 'Modern Problems: Traditional Solutions: Climate Change/Water & Food Security: An Experience of Tarun Bharat Sangha'. Available at http://www.indiawaterportal.org/sites/indiawaterportal.org/files/Rajendra

Sinha, J., Sinha, M. K., and Adapa, U. 2013. *Flow-River Rejuvenation in India: Impact of Tarun Bharat Sangh's Work*. Stockholm: Swedish International Development Cooperation Agency (SIDA).

Sisodia, M. 2009. *Restoring Hope to a Barren Land: 25 Years of Evolution*. Alwar: Tarun Bharat Sangh.

Reddy, T., and Adolf, B. 2002. *Grain Banks for Food Security in Tribal Villages of Orissa*. Rayagada: Agragamee.

World Food Programme (WFP). 2006. *Food and Nutritional Security: World Food Programme*. Delhi: Lancer.

Conclusions
Development as Democracy

A newly independent country embraced the dominant model of development of its time with an unambiguous hope to take its people out of the web of poverty and entrenched inequality, and to take it forward on a path of progress, prosperity and equality. It envisaged a future free of poverty and social oppression. The grand vision required a grand promise, and that promise was development. A country that had suffered a prolonged period of colonization, was poor and seen as backward, chose modernization as its ambitious post-independent nation-building project. Development was intimately connected with democracy, both in the larger contexts of democratic state as the main actor in development and by combining economic development with social justice in policy and planning. This created aspirations and set the framework for assertion in contexts where inadequacies, gaps and conflicts derailed the democratic agenda of development. These assertions articulating rights and social justice for the poor and socially marginalized have pitched to make development democratic. The villages in India are witness to people mobilizing to infuse development with the promises it makes; they are also witness to people filling development with new imagining, new meaning and new values.

The growth model based on the pillars of 'sacrifice' and 'trickle down' has faced resistance from the poor. Development, in this version, asks for 'sacrifice' of some so the larger economic interest of a nation can be served. Invariably, it is the poor who sacrifice. Development does not pretend that the poor will be the first to get the benefit; it assumes that the benefits will 'trickle down' in the long run. When very model of development is based on the pillars of sacrifice and trickle-down effect, it is bound to make development exclusionary and non-distributive. It is not only that the poor are not counted in designing development, but development has been made possible by excluding the poor. Exclusion in this case is by design. The protest movements in many regions of India are articulation of unwillingness of the poor to sacrifice their livelihood resources of land, water and forest for development that does not benefit them.

'Public good' conceptualized as national good that lies at the core of India's planned development has been contested to the extent that national good is no longer synonymous with public good. The extractive model of economic growth followed through successive Five Year Plans has displaced the poor from their homes and fields, and has taken away their subsistence resources of land, water and forests to generate wealth that has resulted in the enclaves of prosperity at the cost of exclusion of the poor for whom saving their resources from encroachment has become a continuous and arduous struggle. In the beginning, it was believed that those displaced by development projects could be resettled and rehabilitated. That, however, has proved to be an unachievable goal. The planners did not learn from years of pursuing industrialization through mining, dams, power projects, etc., against the resistance they faced from people. In seven decades of economic growth, the issues of displacement have not been resolved, and they have escalated in the recent times as the pursuit of economic growth has turned even more ruthless under a neoliberal economy. The poor, seen as obstacles to growth, have, however, learnt from their experience and, instead of negotiating for resettlement, decided to save their resources and reject the growth projects. The sites of growth projects, particularly mining, dams and SEZs, have become vulnerable and conflict-ridden. In this version of development, development and the poor now occupy opposite sides.

The poverty reduction projects are designed to save the poor from the fallouts of economic growth and reduce poverty through welfare, social protection and improvement of the ecological resource base of the poor. The projects per se, however, are no guarantee that the benefits will reach them. The success of the projects has remained localized, resting on a host of local factors such as friendly officials, effective decentralization or social mobilization pushing for effective delivery. The struggle against institutional bias, corruption, bureaucratic control and social powers often entangle the poor in a vicious circle. The villages display the desperation of people who frequent various offices and negotiate with the officials to get included in the projects and get the benefits. Accessing developmental benefits for bare survival thus becomes a struggle. In such cases, demanding from the state has taken two prominent routes— through decentralized governance institutions at the local level and through social mobilization often by CSOs. These two processes taking place at the local level often feed into each other.

The Indian development model tries to blend the two opposite and competing trajectories of economic growth and poverty reduction that run parallel to and are perpetually at war with each other, for they compete for the same resources to serve different interests that cannot coexist harmoniously. The welfare-oriented projects, though critically required, are designed to protect the mere survival of the poor and to save them from falling into despondency and death. Allocation of degraded and wasteland to the poor whether land is allotted as a part of land reforms or as livelihood projects shows how redistribution equals to giving the poor the minimum of resources. Thrown out by the growth model, the poor try to survive by accessing whatever resources the poverty reduction programmes can bring them. The poor, however, do not pin all their hope either on the state or state-led development. They put their energies, knowledge and meagre resources in organizing their own small-scale localized economies. They do not surrender to the despondency that development creates by pushing them outside of the mainstream economy. The economies that the poor build as survival economies are instances of alternatives that have emerged, and still emerging, to an economic mode that pushes them outside its sphere by taking away their resources. The alternative economies founded on the principles of solidarity, equity and respect for ecology illustrate an economic mode that can be egalitarian and inclusive. The politics of natural resources constitute a critical core of development and, consequently, the politics of democratization addresses this in a variety of ways. If rejection of growth model and assertion over resources constitute one stream of democratization of development, accessing, improving and using the resources in an ecological and inclusive manner constitute the other stream.

The acts of democratization of development have stirred the field of development in ways that even the ardent champions of development had not imagined. In the face of exclusion, protests, both large scale and localized, have become crucial not only to seek inclusion but have also defined what inclusion means in specific contexts. If the rejection of a model of development defines inclusion in one context, saving the distributive aspects from being hijacked by the powerful defines inclusion in another. If people get self-organized to resist the powers that deny them access to development, they also participate in the state-institutions at the local levels to counter the powers. If large-scale protest movements broaden the struggle against economic growth, localized CBOs of women, tribal and Dalit engage in everyday struggle to access the welfare provisions of development. The CBOs formed through various state sponsored programmes or by CSOs act as collectives articulating the interests of the marginalized.

In their struggle to democratize development, the mobilization of *identities* has proved to be a potent weapon of the weak—people mobilize by using state-given identities such as SCs, STs, women, landless, small farmers, marginal farmers, BPL households, etc., as well as by constructing identities blending the state-given identities with their own construction of identities that pitch their struggle vis-à-vis development such as *adivasi–kisan–mazdoor* as the Narmada Movement articulates. The *language* of the state occupies a significant place in development, and dealing with this language is strategic to democratize development. The language of the state is either discarded and filled with the language of people articulating an alternative to an extractive and dominant model of development or the language of the state is appropriated, learnt and used to make people's demands comprehensible to the state.

The state comes across as the most dominant actor in development. It is wrongly assumed that the state has withdrawn under neoliberalism. On the contrary, the state's presence is felt more starkly because it is now the facilitator of ruthless neoliberal economic growth. The social contract of industrialization is negotiated by the state as the state acquires land for industries. If the state has an oppressive presence in the arena of economic growth, it has a benign presence in poverty reduction programmes that are directly opposite to the growth projects. The state institutions responsible for the implementation of policies often sabotage them; yet, in the instances where the state responds positively to policies, they facilitate the inclusion of the poor. The state, however, is guided by its commercial interests despite its pro-poor policies. While it grants land rights to the poor, it does not hesitate to take away their land for industrial purposes. While it protects and conserves natural resources such as forests as livelihood resources, it allows the forests to be destroyed for growth projects such as mining. The state only occasionally tries to reach out to citizens; negotiation for inclusion and access to the benefits of development invariably take place in the state's own domain, in its office premises.

Participatory governance through the decentralization of the state has brought the state closer to people. This, on the one hand, has located the state in the same physical setting where people live and, on the other, has turned the state into a social power resulting in competition among social groups for access to and alliance with the state. Participatory governance has given rise to 'new citizen politics' at the village level for the negotiation of power and access to development schemes, and the stirrings at the local level are challenging the old orders of power. While the institutions have brought the hitherto powerless groups into the space of the state, the institutions per se don't guarantee that the poor and socially marginalized get better access to development, or that development becomes inclusive of their interest until the poor mobilize themselves.

The institutions can officially accommodate members as representatives and, when under pressure, can create access to development, but the institutions per se do not guarantee the substantive inclusion of the marginalized. The institutions are weak in the face of the state when it comes to economic growth as they can be bypassed and superseded. Even though there are occasional interventions from other agencies of the state such as the judiciary to reinstate the powers given to the local institutions, their power remains limited. Participatory governance thus contains possibilities as well as limitations in making development democratic. Participatory governance is necessary but not sufficient to foster participation and inclusion or ensure redistribution and equity.

While the state is a power that both the dominant and the weak seek to make alliances with, it has an inclination to seek alliance with the powerful. Much of development thus gets vitiated due to the alliances the state makes. The instances where the state comes forward to align with the poor, the efforts are largely the result of individual officials such as a BDO, a DFO, a gram pradhan or a JE rather than the institutions of the state.

Much of the struggle for democratization of development takes place within the sphere of civil society, although the state remains a central reference point due to its presence and its role in development. The state sometimes works with the actors in civil society mobilizing the poor to place demands on its own institutions. When working towards the implementation of policies, CSOs translate the language of the state, equip people with information about development programmes, make development intelligible, help them articulate demand and pressure the state to deliver development as promised. When contesting policies as social movements, they break the language of the state, bring in other articulation, redefine development and bring pressure on the state to yield to people's demands. While the former works towards inclusion in the existing programmes of development and access to its benefits, the latter protests for the withdrawal of a version of development considered by people a threat to their livelihoods and their very existence. We also find a third type of initiative that creates alternatives for people who are bypassed by the state-sponsored development. In their different manifestations, civil society actions democratize development by countering exclusion, fostering inclusion, and articulating and creating alternatives for the poor and socially marginalized.

It is in the sphere of civil society that the liberal citizen, the lone individual, gets connected to the state through a collective expression of demands and interests. Civil society actions address the powers contained in both the state and the wider society. Democratization of development thus involves reforming both the powers of the state and the social powers. As the two sets of powers often act in alliance, countering one essentially means countering the other, and reforming one has positive consequences for reforming the other. While it may appear that civil society actions are only responses to the state behaviour, it is only partially true. Civil society also sets the context for state behaviour, more so during the articulation for new rights. Once rights are legalized and shift to the domain of the state, the state begins to control the behaviour of civil society.

In the Indian planning of development, economic development is combined with social justice as interrelated goals of development. In the Indian experience of development, social justice has surfaced as both a prerequisite of economic development and its outcome. In the contexts of entrenched inequality, as the land rights case demonstrates, without minimum social equality, economic development for the poor and socially marginalized is an unequal battle with the socially and economically powerful. Even though development in the form of redistribution aims at promoting social justice, accessing redistribution is not possible for people who have highly unequal relations with the powerful.

The institutions through which development is delivered are crucial for social justice. Economic development can enable fight for social justice though the institutions through which development is pursued can limit the fight. The poor and the socially marginalized may access various development provisions such as house, road, water and electricity through schemes designed for them. That, however, does not necessarily lead to social equality. While economic development levels the playing fields for the lower castes and enhances their social status and widens the social space to some extent, the core of social relations revolving around caste does not change. The institutions limit the scope of social justice by defining it in terms of material development. In addition to that, the institutions, when they remain closed to the possibilities of inclusion of socially marginalized as equal members, limit the ability of development to modernize social relation.

A critical facet of democratization of development is contestations over resources, and such contestations are invariably contestation over *rights*. The struggles to save land, water and forests from encroachment by the forces of rampant economic growth are not merely struggles about livelihoods; they are also struggles that speak about rights of poor people over their subsistence resources. The contention is not only about how such rights are not recognized or are inadequately recognized by the formal processes of law but also that these rights can be taken away by invoking another set of laws. It is easy for the state to remove people from what is called 'government land' even if people have been using that land for decades, and no legal claim can be made because people never possessed that land in the legal sense. Even the land people legally possessed can be taken away with the enactment of a law for public good.

Rights from people's perspective thus go beyond the nomenclature of rights as understood in the legal sense. It requires a new language to understand what people mean by rights when they claim their resources such as forests that they don't possess legally, but which is a source of livelihood. The new language of rights transcends the state framework of rights and articulates a worldview from a perspective that is different from the state. It is about honouring the ways of living and choices that are not in line with the views of development and the state.

If the articulation of new rights mark the resistance to growth, articulation of state-given rights mark the access to welfare and poverty eradication projects. In the Indian discourse on development, the language of rights emerged slowly and became more vocal and vociferous with the rights-based framework of development. NREGA put that framework squarely on the map of development thus turning the hitherto beneficiaries of state patronage into right bearing citizens. Even though in the eyes of the state the poor are still benefices of government projects, the struggles to get those benefits are pitched in the language of rights.

A key element emerging from the struggles to democratize development is the desire for *dignity*—the right to live with dignity and the right to be treated with dignity. The experiences of development have brought to the forefront the indignity development has created for those who are at the lowest rung of the socio-economic hierarchy. Whether development extracts people's resources or makes it difficult to access the benefits of development, it intensifies the already prevalent indignities people suffer. Dignity has thus become a critical element of democratization of development: For development to be democratic, it has to bring dignity to those who it intends to benefit. Dignity, a term absent in the lexicon of both development and democracy, is emerging as an aspiration from the encounter between development and the marginalized populace. The aspiration for dignity manifests in myriad ways—respect for the ways of living of the poor, respect for their rights, dignity in access to development, dignity in distribution of development provisions and dignity in equality and equity.

Making development non-violent constitutes one of the key agendas of struggle for rights and social justice. Development, notwithstanding the progressive position it articulates, is not without violence. If the economic growth aspect of development wants to eliminate the worldview of a particular set of population and eliminate people if they resist development, development as poverty eradication and redistribution violates the poor through state control and power unleashed by the state and social forces that often work in collusion. Democratization of development seeks to address and erase violence by rejecting a model of development that has power and violence at its core, and, where people want development to work for them, they attempt to stop violence through confrontation and negotiation with the powers that perpetrate violence. Violence of development signifies the powers that shape development, and rescuing development from violence is to shift the equations of power either by rejecting development altogether or by interrogating violence.

If the dominant model of development has survived despite the discontents, violence, inequities and indignities it has given rise to, it is largely due to the paradoxes it has created. The experiences of power and powerlessness, promise and betrayal, and inclusion and exclusion simultaneously capture the imagination of people. They oppose development of certain kind and want to access development of another kind. It is this duality of development anchored by the duality of the state that saves development from losing its value completely and saves the state from losing its legitimacy as the planner and executor of development. Just at the time when multinational mining companies threaten the resources of the poor, policies such as NREGA and food security boost optimism because the instances where it includes people in the benefits, it provides the much needed hope to people. The success stories do not replace the stories of despair, but they make the despair bearable in anticipation of an imagined or real benefit. That, however, does not keep people blind to the extractive and exclusionary aspects of development. Democratizing development, as evident in the Indian villages, is about rejecting what is not desirable and harnessing what is desirable. Both these processes can take place in the same location, turning the location into a theatre where these two opposite processes take place simultaneously attempting to bring democracy to development.

What this book shows is that the process of democratization of development is an enduring aspect of development. It is never complete. Big gains accrue only occasionally to struggles pitching rights and social justice. Sometimes the results are a series of small gains, and sometimes the results emerge after a prolonged period of struggle. The outcomes are often localized, and the success of a process in one location does not guarantee that it will be successful in another locations. Even the success of a process does not guarantee that it will be sustainable. The equations of power are dynamic in nature, and they are never settled once and for all. What the mobilizations do, in their various forms, is they give power to the marginalized citizens to question and contest what is undemocratic in development. To make development yield results for them, the marginalized populace are required to be in constant vigil and be prepared to wage the struggle when required.

In reaction and response to the universal and unilineal path to progress that development prophesizes, the poor and socially deprived, through their lived experiences of encounters with development, provide multiple versions of the idea of progress and modernity. Despite development's articulation, insistence and imposition of a single notion of modernity, people experience it differently—they resist some forms of modernity; they accept modernity in other forms; and they articulate new versions of modernity through articulation of new rights. Alteration of their existing economic and social relations constitutes the key to modernity. Taking cognizance of people's preferences and articulations reveals modernity as nuanced and defined by a heterogeneous population in their specific locations.

People's struggles vis-à-vis development provides multiple narratives about how those living on the margins of society and economy deal with the might of development that is backed by powerful institutions with an enormous investment of resources. The democratization of development through the infusion of democratic principles and practices of inclusion, equity, participation, redistribution, values of non-violence, dignity and respect for ecology indicates how the poor from their lived experiences of encounter with development are reimaging development to be. If development ever needs redesigning, the script written by the poor in the Indian villages will serve as an important reference point.

Index

About the Author

Ranjita Mohanty is a social scientist based in Delhi. She has been working for past 20 years with a cross-section of institutions that include universities, research organizations, grassroots groups, bilateral and multilateral organizations, thus combining research with policy and practice. Her research covers a wide range—development, social policy, participation, social exclusion and inclusion, civil society, citizen action, and rights and entitlements.

Ranjita Mohanty has a PhD from the Centre for the Study of Social Systems, Jawaharlal Nehru University, New Delhi. Dr Mohanty has held several positions including Fulbright Senior Research Fellow, University of North Carolina, Chapel Hill, USA; Visiting Fellow, University of Western Cape, Bellville, Cape Town, South Africa. She has coedited two books, *Does Civil Society Matter? Governance in Contemporary India* and *Participatory Citizenship: Issues of Identity, Exclusion, Inclusion*, both published by SAGE.